GOD IS WITH US

A TEACHER DEVOTIONAL

DRU COX PEARCY

GOD IS WITH US

A TEACHER DEVOTIONAL

XULON PRESS

Xulon Press
2301 Lucien Way #415
Maitland, FL 32751
407.339.4217
www.xulonpress.com

Paperback ISBN-13: 978-1-66282-827-0
Ebook ISBN-13: 978-1-66282-828-7

King James Version primary source, New International Version, Amplified Version

ACKNOWLEDGEMENTS

I want to thank Lori Taylor for taking time to discuss the process that she went through to get a book published. She took time to answer questions and share information multiple times. Thank you for encouraging me along the way.

I want to thank my small group of prayer warriors for praying and giving me feedback on the devotions that I shared throughout the school year.

I am grateful for Matt, my husband, who has been my continual support.

What Readers Have Said About the Devotions Included in *God Is with Us*

"The devotionals forced me to take an extra minute with God. They helped me refocus on the little things, recognizing that God works in so many different ways and each way is equally important. I would recommend it to someone else! In teaching we can get so caught up in the "one more thing" that was added each day. These would be a great way to start each school day. Just another reminder that God is working through us and we need to take time to appreciate the small moments." Intermediate SPED teacher - Allison

"Dru is a great teacher, friend, and Christ follower who writes devotions that bring Bible truths and real-life teaching experience together. These devotions can be tucked away and read anywhere and anytime one needs a reminder of God's love and how he works in us. Her devotions bring an eagerness to want to read more." - Karen

"Your devotionals are amazing and so wonderfully written. God speaks through you!" – Kindergarten teacher - Janet

"The benefits I received was a particular focus and purpose for that day. Instead of praying for patience, or understanding, or whatever a large all-encompassing topic may be- the devotionals made it more specific and challenged me each day to recognize the good and not dwell too much on the negatives." Intermediate HA Math Teacher – David

"Your writings inspire me and lead me to find quiet moments to remember why we do what we do and who we do it for. You have been a blessing in my life, and I know this book will bring peace and comfort to those who lean on it for guidance in their daily life." K-4 Building Principal – Kevin

INTRODUCTION

WHY I TEACH

Unfortunately, there is a lot of negativity going on in the education world. Teachers are under a lot of scrutiny. Articles of all sorts are being written mostly about the inadequacies of our educational system. Most teachers are insulted by the accusations and rightfully so. The public seems to be generalizing about all public-school teachers. Being judged and portrayed as inadequate in the classroom doesn't do much for the climate of our profession. For the most part, educators feel underappreciated and underpaid. With cutbacks, larger class sizes, and less incentives teachers are considering other options. I have heard more and more teachers say, "It's time for me to retire!" "If I didn't need my health insurance, I would retire." "If I could find another job, I would leave this profession in a heartbeat." It's a sad commentary, but I understand it. I must admit I grow weary myself at times. When I'm down and discouraged, I've had similar thoughts.

God always has a way of giving me a glimmer of hope. When I step away and think about God's calling and His purpose in my life, then I'm grateful for the ministry that He has given me.

I have asked myself several times, "Why teach?" I always come to this conclusion:

***It's God's will for my life and the greatest calling*.**

Teaching is God's greatest calling for me. I have the best job in the world. I see it as a gift from God. It is God's will for my life, and I see it as the best way for me to please my Heavenly Father. Each of us has a calling and mine is teaching. Paul wrote, Ephesians 4:1, "..that ye walk worthy of the vocation wherewith ye are called,.."

***It is full of benefits*.**

Contrary to popular belief, I don't teach for the money. It is not a lucrative job, but it has benefits beyond belief. I teach to make a difference and when I grow discouraged God has a way of reminding me why I teach. It can be a simple breakthrough for a child in class, a smile, fist pump, and/or even a high five when a child receives his or her best grade in class, even if it's not an A. It can be the first time that a timid child asks a question without feeling silly for asking and then when she continues to ask questions more frequently in class. A fifth grader giving me a humble handmade card with a pen-drawn heart on the front saying, "I love you," which melts my heart. My riches are innumerable. They are "my kids."

When "my kids" from past years touch base with me, I'm reminded once again of why I teach. I'm encouraged by letters, visits, a few notes from seniors at the end of their high school career, a Facebook friend request, or an invitation to a graduation. Recently, out of the blue, I received a surprise visit from a former student. The big burly junior came after school and surprised me. We hugged and he told me after looking at his elementary yearbooks that he missed me and just had to come and visit. We caught up on the things that are happening in his life and discussed possibilities of him going to college to be a teacher. That made my day! Within a week or two, I received two letters from former students. I got teary eyed as usual and was once again reminded of why I teach. One of those students wrote, "I remember that you never gave up on me and hoped for the best for my life." You're one of the most inspirational people I've ever known…" "..I want to thank you for inspiring me to chase my dream…"

Old letters from "my kids" of past classes remind me of why I teach. I'm sure their high school teacher gives them a format to follow so they usually tell me what they are doing in high school. Occasionally, they will thank me for helping them be successful in a specific academic area. The one or two sentences that mean the most are sentences that reflect on their memory of me. One girl remembered how important it was in my classroom to be respectful. Another wrote, "You have influenced me to want to become a teacher. You love kids and being around them. I cannot remember you ever being mad at our class." (I'm glad that she couldn't remember a time when I got mad at her class. I'm sure I expressed my frustration at times. It was a challenging group of kids.)

Another young lady reminded me how she struggled in math. She was glad that I would never give up on her. The one statement that stood out to me, "I remember how important honesty was to you. You taught us always to be truthful. I try to live by that." That's why I teach!

***It's my way of honoring the Father*.**

The Bible says in 1 Corinthians 10:31b, "... whatsoever ye do, do all to the glory of God." I don't stand in front of my class and preach the Bible. However, I do not hesitate to let students know what I do on Sundays when I'm asked. When we share our favorite books, I let them know that my very favorite book is the Bible. I make it a practice to live by God's principles, so I emphasize life values and insist that we follow them in my classroom. Jesus taught with love and compassion. I choose to honor Him by following His example.

I was humbled by this e-mail years ago from a student's mother: "Well, Evans Sunday school teacher took me aside at church. They had been talking about how you can still have God with you in school even if school does not allow it by the little things you do. She said Evan raised his hand and said my teacher trusts in the Lord. They can take God out of school but they did not take him out of Mrs. Pearcy." That's why I teach!

I thought my testimony as a 22-year veteran teacher may give a glimpse of my heart and perspective as a Christian teacher. *God Is with Us* was written to encourage teachers to follow God's calling and His ways in their classroom and life.

TABLE OF CONTENTS

Section 1 –
Anticipate & Be Equipped

Anticipate & Be Equipped

Butterflies in the Stomach

"But as it is written, Eye hath not seen, nor ear heard, neither have entered into the heart of man, the things which God hath prepared for them that love him."

1 Corinthians 2:9

A sleepless night precedes the first day of school with students. Butterflies fill the stomach with great anticipation, not from fear but pure excitement of meeting a classroom full of new students for the first time. I remember typing an introductory letter to my fourth-grade students a few years back. The best way to explain my feelings was with "butterflies in my stomach."

Nehemiah, the prophet, had a sleepless night as he surveyed the ruins of Jerusalem. He didn't dwell on the ruins but upon how to rebuild the walls and gates of the city. He was eager to gather the people the next morning with the plan of rebuilding and sharing what God had put in his heart. He had dreamed and planned for the refurbishment of Jerusalem for Jehovah's sake and was anxious to get started.

The thrill as a teacher is allowing oneself to dream of what God has prepared for the new school year. Being excited to complete each goal and to make a difference in each child's life. The blessings and promises that Christ has fulfilled in the past are fuel enough to anticipate more of God's unending grace. It has been my experience that every year brings new challenges and opportunities to grow. I look forward to all that God has for me and "my students."

"But grow in grace, and in the knowledge of our Lord and Saviour Jesus Christ." 2 Peter 3:18

Dear Lord Jesus,

Thank You for the opportunity to touch students' lives. I'm excited to start a new school year and look forward to all that You have prepared. I choose to teach with a zeal that is contagious to my students. May their appetite for learning increase as I motivate and set expectations. Bless each one and help us grow this year in knowledge and grace. In Your precious name I pray, Amen.

Bible Reading – Nehemiah 2

NOTES

Anticipate & Be Equipped

Your Name Matters

"... and he calleth his own sheep by name, and leadeth them out." *John 10:3b*

Roll call in my sixth-grade music class placed a mark on my life. As in every other class, our first and last name was called off. It was the first time that I recall a teacher asking if we preferred another name. I was shy, and I recall my friends encouraging me to tell her my name.

"Drusilla Cox," read the teacher from the class roster.

"My name is Dru. I go by Dru."

"Drew? That's a boy's name," was her unthinkable response.

I start each new school year with that snippet of my life. I tell students that if someone calls me Drusilla, then they don't know me on a personal level. I want to build a personal relationship with my students, and that starts by knowing them by their preferred name. I want them to know that their name matters to me. Name tags and class lists are not permanent until I have every child's preferred name. I have them pronounce it and spell it out if it is a nickname. On the second day of school, name tags reflect the name that makes each child feel at home.

Moses and God had a special relationship. In Exodus 33, Moses found grace in the sight of the Lord, and He knew him by name. His name mattered because there was a relationship between them. Our Good Shepherd knows us by name! He knows me and you personally, and there is great comfort in knowing that my name matters to Him. As we know our Shepherd, be assured that He knows us even better and calls us by name!

"...I know thee by name, and thou hast also found grace in my sight." Exodus 33:12b

Dear Heavenly Father,

Thank You for loving me and being my Good Shepherd. I am grateful that I have a personal relationship with You and am known by my name. Your acceptance of me gives me peace. I trust that You will help me develop relationships with my students that will give them comfort and peace. Assure them of my care when I call them by name.

May Your love be present in all that I say and do. In Jesus's name, Amen.

Reading Text – John 10

Notes

Anticipate & Be Equipped

Five Smooth Stones: Vision

"Where there is no vision, t he people perish..."

Proverbs 29:18a

Years ago, on the first day of each school year our corporation would have staff members gather in the high school auditorium to listen to a motivational speaker. I do not recall the speaker's name, but I do remember the topic: David and Goliath. Each of us received a smooth stone as we entered the auditorium. The speaker asked the audience if we knew how many stones David put in his scrip as he approached the giant, Goliath. Five smooth stones were gathered so that David could kill Goliath and his brothers, too. Our speaker used the story to present five major points to motivate us to meet any challenge that we might face. I'm not sure the exact points that were made, but they could have been vision, wisdom, strength, confidence, and integrity.

Stone One – Vision:

David was criticized for stepping up and showing a willingness to fight Goliath. His oldest brother accused him of being overconfident and evil. David responded, "Is there not a cause?" He recognized the challenge and was not afraid to meet the giant head-on. He knew God would deliver Goliath into his hand just like he did a bear and a lion. He saw this challenge as an opportunity to defend his people and God. Without a vision, which included God's hand in the matter, Goliath and his brothers would not have been defeated.

What is your vision for this school year? With every new school year there are great possibilities and new opportunities. Each year has its challenges. However, if we start with a dream and hold on to it, we will be more likely to approach our challenges as opportunities to fulfill our vision for Christ's sake and to the benefit of our students. Sling that stone of vision in the power of His might!

"And David said, "What have I now done? Is there not a cause?" 1 Samuel 17:29

Dear Heavenly Father,

Thank You for champions like David in the Bible. He wasn't afraid to take the risk of fighting Goliath because he trusted in You. As this new year begins, I claim Your victory because my students are precious in Your sight. There is a cause, and my dream is that all of them will benefit from my teaching. May they see Your love and compassion through me this year. In Jesus' name, Amen.

Bible Reading – 1 Samuel 17

NOTES

Anticipate & Be Equipped

Five Smooth Stones: Wisdom

"Happy is the man that findeth wisdom,
and the man that getteth understanding."

Proverbs 3:13

Tears filled the morning work each of the first five days of fourth grade for one troubled student. It was my first full year of teaching and nothing in a book could have prepared me for such a start to my career. All the strategies and teaching methods in my special education course did not help. Granted, there were expert strategies and solid teachings in that course. For many students, those strategies would have worked. I did not discount the methods, but I truly prayed and called upon the Lord for wisdom concerning him almost daily. By the end of the year, I was given one of his treasured train cars because he wanted me to remember him. How could I forget?

Stone Two – Wisdom:

When David told King Saul that he would fight Goliath, the king gave David the appropriate equipment (his armor) for going to battle. David tried Saul's armor, but it did not fit. (1 Samuel 17:38-40) Five smooth stones, a sling, a shepherd bag, and his scrip was all that David needed. David considered a warrior's way of approaching the enemy, but he was discerning and used what had been successful for him in the past. He was wise in his choice, and God blessed Him in his venture.

Whether a first-year teacher or a veteran, you have been trained to teach and have the knowledge and understanding to do so. The challenge comes in putting into practice that which in theory should be effective. Wisdom is the ability to act using your knowledge, experience, and understanding for specific classroom situations. Having sound judgement in what to say or do when dealing with students can be quite challenging. Be discerning and seek the wisdom of the Lord. Sling that stone of wisdom in the power of His might!

"So that thou incline thine ear unto wisdom, and apply thine heart to understanding;" Proverbs 2:2

Dear Heavenly Father,

Thank You for the training and support You have provided for me to make good decisions. Bring to remembrance good counsel that will assist in my interactions today. Help me to be wise in the decisions that I make as I work with students today. I choose to be in tune with Your guidance. I lean on You fully. In Jesus's name, Amen.

Bible Reading – Proverbs 2

NOTES

Anticipate & Be Equipped

Five Smooth Stones: Strength

"...for the joy of the LORD is your strength."

Nehemiah 8:10

Stone three – Strength:

There is excitement and joy as the new school year starts. We start with an engine full of steam and vitality. We are at full strength and ready to conquer the world. Our goals and dreams are all within reach. Everyone gets settled in. The day-to-day student challenges begin to drain our strength and joy. Parents can be demanding and challenging, too. I learned early in my teaching career that the key to maintaining my strength was to put Jesus first, others next, and me third. I am reminded of this simple song from Sunday school:

J-O-Y
Jesus and others and you,
What a wonderful way to spell joy.
Jesus and others and you,
In the heart of each girl and each boy.
J is for Jesus, so give Him first place.
O is for others, we meet face to face.
Y is for you, so whatever you do.
Put yourself third and spell joy.
(B. Metzger - 1951) [1]

In 1 Samuel 17:45 – 47, David declared that the victory was the Lord's. He acknowledged that it was not in his own strength but "in the name of the Lord," "the LORD deliver thee into mine hand;" and "… the battle is the LORD'S.." David drew his courage and strength by putting God first.

When giving God daily pre-eminence, we become empowered with His strength to love the unlovely and meet all challenges that we face. After all, the joy of the Lord is our strength, so acknowledge Jesus Christ first, consider others second, and love yourself thirdly. Sling that stone of strength in the power of His might!

---

[1] Metzger. *Jesus and Others and You*. Ohio: The Lorain County Free-Net Chapel, 2015. www.childrenschapel.org/biblestories/sheetmusic/joysong.html

"That he would grant you, according to the riches of his glory, to be strengthened with might by his Spirit in the inner man;" Ephesians 3:16

Dear Heavenly Father,

Thank You for being my strength. I know that I can do all things because You give me strength. When I grow weary in my work with children and adults, help me to draw my strength from You. Help me to always put You first, look to the needs of others next, and then take less offense in what others say or do to me. This year is mine to conquer because I have You. Bless it for Your honor and glory. Amen.

Bible Reading – Psalm 16

NOTES

____

____

____

____

____

____

Anticipate & Be Equipped

Five Smooth Stones: Confidence

"Being confident of this very thing, that he which hath begun a good work in you will perform it until the day of Jesus Christ:"

Philippians 1:6

In fourth grade, I had the best teacher ever. I was shy and so backward that I peed my pants during a spelling bee in her classroom. She quietly took care of me and was always so kind. My uncle passed away that year, and she was so thoughtful and nurturing during a sad time in my life. I knew as a ten-year old that I wanted to be a teacher just like her.

Smooth Stone Four:

David had gained confidence in God in the fields against the bear and the lion. When he approached Goliath, he didn't appear to be any threat to Goliath. David had all the confidence in the world that the Lord would deliver Goliath into his hand. He boldly proclaimed, "This day will the LORD deliver thee into mine hand; and take thine head from thee; ..." (1 Samuel 17:46a) David remembered God's faithfulness and he defeated Goliath that day.

God called me to teach at a young age, and I was given opportunity as a teenager to teach in our Sunday school. My confidence grew over time as I saw God touch the lives of the boys and girls that I taught. Confidence was gained by experiencing success and knowing that my love for teaching originated with God's call in my life. When I feel defeated, I remember that God will perform in and through me as I yield to Him. He has been faithful!

The challenge of teaching and life is real but as Lysa TerKeurst says, "Tonight, no matter what you're going through... backtrack and remember all the places where God has been so faithful before in your life. And know. Know with assurance. And boldness. And confidence. He is the same faithful God."[2] Sling that stone of confidence in the power of His might!

"Seek the LORD, and his strength: seek his face evermore. Remember his marvellous works that he hath

[2] TerKeurst, Lisa, Facebook post, October 27, 2014, http://www.azquotes.com/quote/878372

done; his wonders, and the judgments of his mouth." Psalm 105:4-5

Dear Lord Jesus,

Thank You for Your faithfulness to me. I know my confidence comes from seeing Your hand in my life. I praise You for the courage to meet the challenges of this life. My confidence is in You, the One who has called me to teach. When I doubt, remind me of Your marvelous works. Thank You for working in and through me. In Your name I pray, Amen.

Bible Reading – Philippians 1

NOTES

Anticipate & Be Equipped

Five Smooth Stones: Integrity

"The integrity of the upright shall guide them…"

Proverbs 11:3a

My first professional interview came when I was 38 years old. I sat in front of a panel of three principals at a large table. We said our hellos, and I explained that I had never been interviewed before but would answer their questions as best as I could. I didn't know all the right terms or have much classroom experience. So, I shared my heart and life experiences that I felt would help meet the needs of students in the classroom. I was honest! When the interview was over, I recall one principal looking at me with a grin and saying, "So you've never interviewed before?" Before the day was over, I was offered the job.

When my principal retired a few years later, she told me that she hired me because of my interview. "I couldn't tell you before, but the reason I hired you was because I knew you were a Christian," she smiled.

Stone Five: Integrity

David was genuine and sincere in his willingness to conquer the giant, Goliath. In 1 Samuel 17:33-37, King Saul questioned David's credentials when he entered his headquarters. David told Saul how he killed a lion and a bear while taking care of his father's sheep. Saul's concern was that he was not a trained soldier, but David's honesty and trust in God convinced King Saul that David was the one that could defeat Goliath.

Honesty is the best policy, and it is biblical. As a new teacher enters her own classroom, she uses the few experiences that she has received in her training. That is what David did in the power of the Lord. As David matured into a warrior, he didn't continue to use a sling and stones. He was able to use the weapons and armor because he learned from those around him. In a survey to veteran teachers, one advice that over half of those teachers gave was "Ask for help." That takes honesty to yourself and others. Use what you know, but be willing to learn from others. Sling that stone of integrity in the power of His might!

"Let integrity and uprightness preserve me; for I wait on thee:" Psalm 25:21

Dear Heavenly Father,

Thank You for being a righteous God that rewards integrity. Forgive me for allowing my pride to keep me from asking for help. I choose to be honest and genuine in all my dealings. May I never forget Your hand and leading in my life. Direct me in ways pleasing to You. In Jesus's name, Amen.

Bible Reading – Psalm 25

NOTES

Section 2 – Friendly Support

Friendly Support
More Is Better

"Wherefore comfort yourselves together, and edify one another, even as also ye do."

1 Thessalonians 5:11

At the beginning of the school year, the students and I have conversations about the positive aspects of working in small groups. Without fail, someone will say more people working together is better because together there are more ideas and more help. They are right, and more is better for believers too.

In Exodus 17, Moses became weary when holding up the rod of God in battle. Moses stood on top of the hill overseeing the battleground as Joshua led the army of Israel. As long as Moses held the rod up in the air Israel would win. Just as soon as he rested his arms, the enemy would win! Aaron and Hur were with Moses. The three men realized that it was important to the outcome of the battle for Moses to keep the rod up in the air. Knowing it was too difficult for Moses to physically keep that rod in the air throughout the entire battle, Aaron and Hur sat Moses on a rock, and then each took hold of an arm and held it up with Moses holding the rod of God in his hands. Being reinforced by Aaron and Hur was necessary because Moses could not do it in his own strength. The battle was won by the Israelites because Moses received the support that he needed to hold the rod of God high in the sky.

In the Christian walk, it is essential that we rely on fellow believers. Some burdens may be so heavy they require an uplifting of friends to endure. Trials and problems endured for a long period of time can be wearisome. Initially, we may think we can handle things on our own. We must come to the realization that we need one another to endure and overcome circumstances and spiritual battles. As Aaron and Hur were supportive and essential in the winning of the battle, our Christian brothers and sisters are important in holding us up in prayer and fellowship.

Is your load too heavy to carry alone? Let your loved ones lift those weighty burdens to the Lord for you. Is there someone who could use your support and prayers? The Bible tells us to pray for, edify, uplift, and love one another. Together we can carry and uplift the heavy arms and burdens of each other to a life of victory and praise.

"Two are better than one;... For if they fall, the one will lift up his fellow:..." Ecclesiastes 4:9a & 10a

Dear Heavenly Father,

Thank You for surrounding me with believing teachers. My burdens are heavy, and I know they are lifting me up in prayer today. As they pray for me, I pray for them. When I try to hide my troubles from others, help me to remember that more is better. Thank You for giving me loving friends and family that faithfully pray for me. Bless them. In Jesus' name, Amen.

Bible Reading – Exodus 17

NOTES

____

____

____

____

____

____

Friendly Support
FRIENDSHIP

"... but I have called you friends; for all things that I have heard of my Father I have made known unto you."

John 15:15b

"What is a friend?" was the topic for our morning circle conversation. Students were anxious to participate.

"A friend is someone you like to be with," one student smiled as she looked at her lunch buddy.

Another student interjected, "They like to play football with me."

"I think it is someone who will listen and not talk behind my back," was another heartfelt response, "and someone you can trust."

Some students struggle to find that genuine friend, but in most cases, they know what they want. True friends can trust and confide in each other. A good friend often uplifts with words of encouragement and comfort. She is willing to help and spend time with you which in turn strengthens the bond of friendship.

Whether from a teacher survey that I gave or my research into the phases of a first-year teacher, the advice was the same: Find someone that you can confide in and rely on when you need help. Our earthly friends are a blessing of God but often are incapable of meeting all our needs. When I think of the qualifications of a perfect friend, there is only one that meets all criteria, Jesus. Think about it!

He is trustworthy and faithful. – Lamentations 3:22-24
He listens, so I can confide in Him. – Psalm 34:17
He is my helper. – Hebrews 13:6
He is my shield and uplifter. – Psalm 3:3
As I get closer to Him, He gets closer to me. – James 4:8

There is no greater friend than Jesus, however, God has placed special people in our lives to be our friends. We need each other and should develop relationships that allow us to freely share our moments of hope and despair. Friends that will laugh with us, cry with us, and pray with us. As we strengthen our friendship with Jesus, may we take time to bond with those who love us and can support us with God's blessing.

"... and there is a friend that sticketh closer than a brother." Proverbs 18:24b

Dear Heavenly Father,

Thank You for being my friend. I choose to obey and seek You diligently. May I be a friend that sticks closer than a sibling and one who uplifts and encourages others. May my words be Your words, and my ways Your ways. Thank You for my lovely friends. Help me to allow them to support me when necessary. For it's in Your name I pray, Amen.

Bible Reading – Proverbs 17

NOTES

FRIENDLY SUPPORT

A MARIGOLD

"Therefore encourage and comfort one another and build up one another, ..."

1 Thessalonians 5:11a (Amp)

"Thank you for being my marigold," one teacher said. "I'm not sure what you mean."

When I looked up the idea of a marigold for myself, I found an article that encouraged new teachers to find a marigold: a teacher that is positive, energetic, and can nurture and help them grow.[3] Marigold flowers are often used to surround a garden of vegetables to protect them from varmints. They also allow the plants to grow to their fullest. Whether a novice or veteran, we need marigolds around us.

---

[3] Gonzalez, Jennifer, "Find Your Marigold: The One Essential Rule for New Teachers", Cult of Pedagogy, Accessed July 19, 2021, www.cultofpedagogy.com/wp-content/uploads/2014/09/Find-Your Marigold.pdf

It was a veteran colleague who complimented me for making a positive impact and helping her grow. I could say the same of her. Later that year, I bought a marigold to give her. On my way to school, the plant dumped and made a mess. I put the dirt back in the pot and reset the plant as best as I could. It was going to need her attention. I was reminded at that moment "this marigold, me" was a mess. As a mentor, I knew my own failures. I needed God's attention and gave Him mine. I asked for forgiveness and thanked Him by God's grace that I could still be a blessing to someone.

The Bible confirms that we need others, and they need us. Paul exhorts us to encourage and uplift others. Be the marigold! Solomon tells us that there is safety in the advice of many. Don't hesitate to ask for help. Find your marigold/s.

"Two are better than one; because they have a good reward for their labour. For if they fall, the one will lift up his fellow: but woe to him that is alone when he falleth; for he hath not another to help him up." Ecclesiastes 4:9-10

Dear Heavenly Father,

Thank You for giving me a support system that is passionate about children and are willing to help me be the teacher that You want me to be. I choose to be a positive impact in a way that pleases You first and foremost. Help me not to be too proud to ask for help when I need it. I choose to grow and improve my art for Your honor and glory. In Jesus' precious name, Amen.

Bible Reading – I Corinthians 13

NOTES

Friendly Support

Whose Got Your Back?

"For where two or three are gathered together in my name, there am I in the midst of them;"

Matthew 18:20

I was grateful when a colleague approached me before the school year started and asked me to lead a Monday morning prayer time. It has been a small group, and at times it has been me and one other person. I remind myself that if there are only two or three of us that meet to pray, Jesus is in the middle of us (Matthew 18:20). Our small group has come to rely on each other for prayers whether we are in attendance or not. As teachers we need to cover each other's backs.

Most of us are familiar with the command to put on the whole armor of God. Each piece of armor is a covering for the front side of the body. If all the pieces cover the front of the body in battle, what about the backside? In battle, soldiers are expected to protect each other. They cover each other's back. In Ephesians 6, after Paul told the saints to put on the whole armor of God, he bids them to pray for each other. As we uplift one another, we are providing the added protection that may be necessary. The support and prayer of our friends and family is the covering for our back as we walk this life of faith.

Once we put on the armor, we need others to pray and cover our backside. We must allow others to enter our life by asking them to pray for us. They may only pray when we ask. Being part of a small prayer group gives us an opportunity to be a prayer warrior for others, as they pray for us. Whenever we need prayer, we know who we can ask for prayer. Do you have others praying for you? It is not a sign of weakness, but necessary for an effective Christian life of faith. Whose got your back?

"...The effectual fervent prayer of a righteous man availeth much." James 5:16b

Dear Heavenly Father,

Thank You for providing all that I need to live a victorious life. I put on the whole armor of God to withstand the devil's tricks. Thank You for surrounding me with

Christian teachers who pray for me as I pray for them. I know they have my back. Even when I've been discouraged, You have provided me the support that I have needed. I know You are with us and choose to support my friends by praying faithfully for them. In Jesus' name, Amen.

Bible Reading – Ephesians 6:18-24

Notes

Friendly Support

Blessed by Association

"He that walketh with wise men shall be wise: but a companion of fools shall be destroyed."

Proverbs 13:20

"Have you ever thought about who you are hanging out with?" I asked a student who had been getting himself in trouble. He was a new student trying to fit in with a mischievous group of boys. By nature, he was kind and softhearted but by association he was developing a bad reputation. By second semester, the boy had a new group of friends. He was thrilled when he and his buddies were given the responsibility of getting the tricycles to and from the building for our trike race practices. His new group of friends had proven themselves to be trustworthy. He was rewarded that privilege because of the dependability of his friends.

According to the Bible, there is blessing by association. In Genesis 30, Laban, Jacob's uncle, admitted that the Lord's blessing (prosperity and success) in his life was because Jacob was with him. God had multiplied all that Laban had during his stay. Jacob was blessed of God and by association, Laban reaped the benefits. In Genesis 39, Joseph, was in captivity. Because of his good character, he was elevated to overseer of Potiphar's house. The Lord blessed that Egyptian's house and fields for Joseph's sake. Even though Joseph was in captivity, God's hand was on everything that he did. Potiphar, the jailor, and Pharaoh all reaped the benefits of God's blessing by their relationship with Joseph.

As a believer in Christ Jesus, others should reap the blessings that we experience as we trust in Him. How much more our blessings as we maintain friendships with fellow believers! Non-believers are in our lives so that we can be a blessing and light for Christ Jesus. Whether we associate with believers or non-believers, may it be said of us, "We are blessed by the Lord because of you."

"Blessed is the man that trusteth in the LORD, and whose hope the LORD is." Jeremiah 17:7

Dear Heavenly Father,

Thank You for blessings from above. Your promises are true and give great hope and peace. I trust You Lord Jesus and choose to point others to You. May my friends and colleagues be blessed as You bless me. I thank You for the friends that enrich my life with Heavenly blessings. May others experience Your blessings like I have. Thank You, Lord Jesus. Amen.

Bible Reading – Genesis 39

NOTES

Friendly Support
Learn from Others

"Brethren, be followers together of me, and mark them which walk so as ye have us for an ensample."

Philippians 3:17

"I'm a good teacher, not a great teacher," was my response to our building's new principal when asked what made me "Teacher of the Year." I appreciated the vote of confidence from my fellow colleagues but knew then and know now that I have not reached my fullest potential.

For years, I have made a practice of visiting other teachers' classrooms. I had been a mentor to one young teacher, and I recognized her knowledge base and strength in literacy. I observed her running literature circles with great success. Her guided conversations were great! A piece of her teaching became a piece of my teaching. Another young colleague allowed me to observe her third graders doing station work. Her organization and expectations were evident in the movement of students, and their full engagement was impressive. A piece of her teaching became a piece of my teaching. A veteran teacher allowed me to observe her class as they worked independently on their creative writing. I listened intently to her conversations with students. A piece of her teaching became a piece of my teaching. Many others have influenced and provided examples of best teaching practices for me throughout the years.

In Philippians 3, Paul said that even with all that he had achieved he had not reached perfection. He was not satisfied to live in the past but strived and pushed himself to reach the prize of the high calling of Christ Jesus. Taking steps to reach God's best, he encouraged the Philippians to find those around them that could provide a good example and practice.

Over the years many teachers, coaches, and principals have contributed to my teaching practices. Their examples and guidance have led to my teaching successes, but I have not yet attained to all that God has for me. I'm still pressing toward God's prize in His calling for me. I encourage you to do the same.

"I press toward the mark for the prize of the high calling of God in Christ Jesus." Philippians 3:14

Dear Lord Jesus,

Thank you for Your many blessings in my life. Help me to be observant of those that can lead me to be a better teacher for Your name's sake. I strive to be pleasing to You. As my colleagues have been examples to me, help me be an example to others. I submit my life and teaching afresh to You and continue to press toward Your best for me. I love You. In Jesus' name I pray, Amen.

Bible Reading – Philippians 3

NOTES

FRIENDLY SUPPORT

SEEKING ANSWERS FROM THE RIGHT SOURCE

"The heart of the righteous thinks carefully about how to answer [in a wise and appropriate and timely way],"

Proverbs 15:28a (Amp)

"I don't have a good grade in science. I'm not sure what to do," wrote one student.

"I can't access Assessment 18. Can you fix it for me?" messaged another student.

"Would you take 10% off morning work for not having one sentence completed?" asked yet another student.

All these messages had come to me six to eight weeks into my medical leave. Other teachers had been teaching those classes, giving assessments, and grading papers. I was glad to hear from my students, but I was not the one to ask. My response in essence was to talk to their current teacher. That was the best that I could do to help.

I wonder if you are seeking advice from those who can truly help you. Who are you messaging or leaning on for advice? Are you seeking comfort from someone who will likely agree with you? Does your friend give you godly counsel? Having good friends to lean on is a blessing, however, sometimes it is best to go directly to the Savior for His guidance in your situation. After all, He is the One who holds the key to all things!

Thankfully, God has provided us with friends who will listen and confide in us. At times, giving friends good advice can be difficult. When they come to ask advice or to vent, how do you guide them? Do you chime in with your two cents worth and a piece of your mind? Do you advise them to go to someone who can answer or do something about their problem? Do you point them to the One who can help them? Ultimately, it is the Holy Spirit who "will guide into all truth," according to John 16:13. If we walk in the Spirit daily with prayer, our responses should benefit our colleagues and be pleasing to God. Sweet counsel brings comfort, especially when given by a fellow believer. It will never be bad advice to direct our friends to the Savior, even if that is all that we have to say.

"Ointment and perfume rejoice the heart: so doth the sweetness of a man's friend by hearty counsel." Proverbs 27:9

Dear Heavenly Father,

Forgive me for seeking everyone else's advice without seeking You first. Today, I choose to rely upon You fully. I'm thankful that You have placed __________ in my life to help direct my paths in this pressing matter. Help me to respond and guide others in a godly way when called upon. I choose to walk in the Spirit and advise others to seek You too. You are my awesome God, and I trust that You will have Your hand in all that I say and do. Your name be honored and glorified today, Amen.

Bible Reading – Proverbs 27

NOTES

____

____

____

____

____

____

FRIENDLY SUPPORT

PIECE OF THE PUZZLE

"For as the body is one, and hath many members, and all the members of that one body, being many, are one body: so also is Christ."

1 Corinthians 12:12

A team cannot function at its fullest without all members contributing. We are all uniquely designed and have been given gifts and talents to use for the glory of God. What can you provide for your team?

- Leadership
- Experience that brings a calm
- Creativity to design presentations
- Organization and planning
- Motivation - cheerleader
- Envision the big picture with enthusiasm
- Focus on the small details to fulfill the big picture
- Insight to help bridge the standards of the prior grade to the current grade level
- Analyze curricula to focus on priority standards

- Adapt team schedule when necessary
- Research resources to share with team
- Technology guru
- Notetaker – timekeeper – keep team on task
- Sense of humor – comedy relief
- Fresh perspective

What do you contribute to your team? Are you actively using your gifts and skills to help complete your team? Maybe you feel unnecessary or under-appreciated, so you don't participate. Maybe you have deceived yourself into thinking you don't need your teammates. Either scenario means that your team is not functioning at its best and neither are you.

In 1 Corinthians 12, Paul addresses the gifts of the church and apparently members felt less or more valued by the gifts that they had. Paul uses an analogy of the body and its parts to help us understand God's design. He puts great emphasis on the fact that every body part is necessary for the body to function at its best. The same is true of the body of Christ.

We are all important in the ministry of Christ. God had given us different gifts and talents. Our uniqueness should be used to help our team function as it is designed. Each of us is import-ant to the well-being of our team of colleagues. Working side by side, we are each an essential piece of the puzzle. Pieced together we create a beautiful picture of God's approved purpose for our lives.

"Be of the same mind one toward another." Romans 12:16a

Dear Heavenly Father,

Thank You for the gift of teaching and the many other skills that You have grown in me. Help me to use them appropriately. May my teammates know that I respect their gifts and talents by my interaction with them. May we work side by side in harmony and please You in our decisions. Thank You for my team! In all that we do or say, may it be pleasing to You. In Jesus' name, Amen.

Bible Reading – 1 Corinthians 12

NOTES

____

____

____

____

____

Friendly Support

Credit Where Credit Is Due

"The Lord recompense thy work, and a full reward be given thee of the Lord God of Israel, under whose wings thou art come to trust."

Ruth 2:12

"I can't imagine teaching the classes I have without the great assistants that I have had," commented one of my colleagues. "I've had some of the best!"

When she began to list a few of her assistants, I had to agree. "They are some of the best!"

The Apostle Paul used an entire chapter to express his appreciation for those who encouraged him and were a part of his ministry. It was the only time that some of them were ever mentioned in the Bible. He wanted them to be remembered. There were at least six of Paul's epistles where he mentioned those that had supported him. Paul understood the importance of giving credit where credit was due.

Without Mary, Trudy, Dawn, Jodie, Brooke, Patty, Sue, Lori, Lisa, Karen, Kelly, Matthew, Hoop, Tracy, Christina, Kristen, Dana, Rebecca, Megan, and Michelle I could not be a successful teacher. My students and I have been better because of them. They have taught, coached, nursed, counseled, encouraged, transported, escorted, intervened, modeled, modified, assessed, and supported me and my students throughout the years. They have sat and worked one on one, led in small groups, modeled writing, and guided in math, co-taught, and so much more. All of them bring their own uniqueness and share my passion for children.

As Paul, we must not forget those who have been so detrimental to our ministry. We must recognize them for the significance of their work. They need to know that we are appreciative and that we value them. Take time to thank them. They are a gift from God!

"I thank my God upon every remembrance of you," Philippians 1:3

Dear Heavenly Father,

Thank You for blessing me with men and women who have supported me throughout the years. Their work and efforts have made a difference in my classroom. Forgive me for not being diligent to thank my assistants as often as I should. Help them to feel appreciated daily as we interact. Bless them for their dedication and love. In Jesus' name, Amen.

Bible Reading – Romans 16

NOTES

SECTION 3 – CLASSROOM PRACTICES

CLASSROOM PRACTICES

FOUR TO ONE

"Pleasant words are as an honeycomb, sweet to the soul, and health to the bones."

Proverbs 16:24

I have a small 4:1 poster in my classroom. I keep it up to remind me to focus on students' positive behaviors rather than the negative. Recognizing and acknowledging the good in students has transformed my outlook and the culture of my classroom.

"Thank you, Johnny for doing your morning work without me reminding you," I say. A smile is the immediate response.

"Kelly, Courtney, Kevin, and Tommy have their supplies out and are ready to go. I can see they are anxious to learn with me. Thank you!" I comment as I prepare to transition to our next activity. Others begin to react and get ready.

Without others hearing, I let Sammy know that I saw him help his struggling classmate. "I'm so proud of you for helping him out," I whisper. He blushes and doesn't know what to say. You can tell he is surprised and pleased that I noticed.

Words of kindness and validation create a congenial environment and are good for the soul. That is scriptural! Not only do the students benefit from good words, but I physically and emotionally feel better about my day. It makes me happy to see boys and girls doing what I ask.

In 2 Chronicles 10:7, "If thou be kind to this people, and please them, and speak good words to them, they will be thy servants forever." That was the advice given by the older men to young King Rehoboam concerning how to treat the Israelites. His father had been a harsh king, and the people were begging King Rehoboam to be different. (That was good advice and yet the young king ignored their counsel.) Kindness and good words will help develop good relationships which in turn will produce teacher-pleasers in your classroom.

"Let the words of my mouth, and the meditation of my heart, be acceptable in thy sight, O Lord, my strength, and my redeemer." Psalm 19:14

Dear Heavenly Father,

As I interact with my students this day, help me to see the good in them. You have told us to think on the things that are true, pure, and of a good report. May my words show Your love and kindness and then result in a good learning experience for all. I trust You to use me this day. In Jesus' name, Amen.

Bible Reading – Proverbs 16

NOTES

Classroom Practices
The Golden Rule

"Therefore all things whatsoever ye would that men should do to you, do ye even so to them:"

Matthew 7:12a

On the first few days of school, students take part in creating the rules for our classroom. Without fail, when we discuss what it looks like to be respectful, someone will say, "Treat others the way you want to be treated." That prompts me to ask the students how they want to be treated.

"I want people to listen when I'm talking," replies one student.

"Be nice and use kind words," another chimes in.

Those and other responses reveal that students have a good grasp of what respect should look like and yet they struggle to be considerate, as do adults. It was in the first couple of weeks of school, I had a student become agitated because his mechanical pencil lead kept breaking. He became so upset about it that he was interrupting the entire class. Once I figured out what was going on, I reached for a pencil on my desk and said, "It's no big deal. Here's another pencil." That only seemed to irritate him more.

After much coaxing, I was able to get him to take a break. Once I finished my lesson and got students started with their seatwork, I went to speak with the student. We had a short conversation, and then he said something that has stuck with me. He said, "Why did you disrespect me by saying, 'It's no big deal'?" I told him that his problem was not a big deal to me but if it was to him, I was sorry for hurting his feelings. (Not everyone's big deal is the same.) He accepted my apology.

Calmly, I asked him, "Why did you disrespect me and your classmates by disrupting our learning? Why did you disrespect me by not following my directions?" At that moment, we made a connection. We gained each other's respect that day because we listened to each other, spoke kindly to each other, and gave each other forgiveness. Living the Golden Rule benefits everyone, and it's Christ-like.

"And be ye kind one to another, tenderhearted, forgiving one another, even as God for Christ's sake hath forgiven you." Ephesians 4:32

Dear Heavenly Father,

Thank You for setting the best example and giving us the Golden Rule. I choose to create a culture of love and kindness with my students and colleagues. Help me to interact with others respectfully. In Jesus' name, Amen.

Bible Reading – Matthew 7:1-12

NOTES

Classroom Practices
A.L.I.C.E. Training

"The angel of the LORD encampeth round about them that fear him, and delivereth them."

Psalm 34:7

An anxious student and his grandmother arrived one day before the school year started to lessen his anxiety. After a tour of the building and practicing his locker, he sat down at his desk to talk with me. He saw that I have two great big windows. Tears began to wail up in his eyes, and his voiced trembled as he said, "That's not safe. What if an intruder comes to our school? He will see us!"

I stepped closer to the young man and assured him that I would protect him. I went through each step that we would take if an intruder entered the building. He had experienced A.L.I.C.E. training in previous grades, and it was evident that he didn't find peace in the plan.

From a teacher's point of view, one of the least favorite trainings of the year is our A.L.I.C.E. training. Facing the possibility of an intruder wanting to cause havoc and harm to students and teachers is disconcerting. You can sense fear and tension in the questions and comments made by staff members. Then we are sent to calmly teach our students, who have their own fears, the strategies (alert, lockdowns, inform, counter, evacuate).[4] Then we practice a lockdown.

There are so many scenarios that play out in my mind when I allow the "what ifs" to control my thoughts. To erase those fears, I lean on God's Word.

I envision an angel of the Lord wrapping its wings around me and my students. – Psalm 34:7

I imagine being in lockdown and hovering over my students with Christ hovering over me like a hen and His shield over all of us. – Psalm 91:3-4

I know that the Lord will preserve me from evil whether I stay inside or lead students to our rally point. – Psalm 121:7-8

Being aware that Christian teachers have died protecting students from their attacker, I commit my life to Christ by saying, "For to me to live is Christ, and to die is gain." – Philippians 1:21 The Lord's will be done!

---

[4] "ALICE Training Video." YouTube video, 8:01. Posted by "hanoverhighhawks." October 15, 2014. https://www.youtube.com/watch?v=x_5wl041T4Q.

As Elisha encouraged his servant in *2 Kings 6:16 "Fear not: for they that be with us are more than they that be with them."* We have angels all around!

> *Dear Lord Jesus,*
>
> *I thank You for being my rock, my fortress, and my bulwark. My faith and hope can only be found in You. There is evil all around. Help me not to dwell on the threat of evil but upon Your goodness and watch care. Protect me, my colleagues, my students, and my entire school family. You are faithful so I place my trust in You afresh today. In Your precious name I pray, Amen.*

Bible Reading – 2 Kings 6:9-17

NOTES

____

____

____

____

____

____

Classroom Practices

Grace

"... that we may obtain mercy, and find grace to help in time of need."

Hebrews 4:16

"Thank you for showing me grace," was a comment that my teaching partner made to me a few days after she revealed a personal failure. She had cried with disappointment in herself. I asked her if she asked God for forgiveness, and of course she had. I reassured her of God's forgiveness and love for her. I hugged her and prayed with her that day. In her mind, that was a picture of God's grace to her!

Since that time, I have been more cognizant to show grace to my students. When a student tells me he is sorry, I respond, "You are forgiven." (I don't tell him that it is alright because his behaviors are not.) Showing genuine grace gives a guilty student forgiveness and freedom to improve. Isn't that what we want from our Savior?

God's grace is sufficient to meet each of our struggles. Be transparent, confide in the Savior, and seek His forgiveness when necessary. God's forgiveness allows us to sense His acceptance and redeeming power. There is a sense of freedom in that, and it is all based upon Christ and Him alone. According to Ephesians 1, we are accepted, redeemed, and forgiven by Christ Jesus. As we have experienced God's grace, we should demonstrate that same grace to our students by accepting and forgiving them.

"And he said unto me, My grace is sufficient for thee:..."
2 Corinthians 12:9a

Dear Heavenly Father,

Thank You for Your unending grace and love. Thank You for Your forgiveness and acceptance. I choose to be gracious to my students as You have showed grace to me. May I never forget how wonderful You have been and are to me. In Jesus' name I pray, Amen.

Bible Reading – Ephesians 1

Notes

Classroom Practices

Does God Accommodate His Children?

"I will have mercy on whom I will have mercy…" Romans 9:15b

Just like many teachers, I have been challenged to deal with children who drum to a different beat. Some struggle with classroom behavior so they have behavior plans that require rewards be given when goals are met. That has been a struggle for me and fellow teachers. How do other students feel when a misbehaved child is rewarded, and they are not?

Students have complained and feel it is unfair when a student who misbehaves a lot in class is rewarded when he finally has a good half day or full day. That seems a bit unfair to them and yet it happens. As I have considered what I have been coached to do with students with severe needs, I have determined that it is the right thing to do. I have wrestled with it and even spoken to others about it. I have prayed and gone to the

Bible to find peace about making accommodations. I asked myself, "Does God accommodate his children?"

Almost immediately the parable of the Prodigal Son came to mind. A wealthy father had two sons. The one son took his inheritance, left home, spent it all, and ended up eating cornhusks with the hogs. When he came to his senses, he returned home hoping to at least be treated like his father's servants. His father was so excited that he had a feast prepared, had the best robe placed on his long-lost son, put a ring on his hand, and shoes on his feet. It appeared that his father was rewarding him for something that he didn't deserve! The older son became very angry and pointed out that he had always been obedient and faithful and yet had never been given a party. The father was not discounting the loyalty and obedience of his oldest son. He didn't love one son above the other. The faithful one was going to be rewarded for his faithfulness, but it wasn't at that point in time. The father was not comparing the works and deeds of his sons nor was he condoning the riotous behavior of his long-lost son. The forgiving father couldn't help but show compassion and celebrate his son's changed heart and his return home. That's accommodation.

"...love covereth all sins." Proverbs 10:12b

Dear Heavenly Father,

Thank You for the privilege of teaching. As I consider the needs of my students, I ask You to give me discernment in all that I do for them. Give me the strength and courage for each challenge. If I give more attention to a student of need, help the other children know that I love them, too. Continue to give me the grace and love to do what is right. Help me to express your love in my words and actions, for every child counts! In Jesus' name, Amen.

Bible Reading – Luke 15:11-32

NOTES

Classroom Practices

What Will I Say?

*"And I have put my words in thy mouth,
and I have covered thee in the shadow of
mine hand,..."*

Isaiah 51:16a

Talking to parents can be one of the most difficult things to do. I've had knots in my stomach when even thinking about the possibility of a confrontation. How do you talk to a parent about her baby's misbehavior and/or incompetence? How do you respond to a nasty e-mail that attacks your integrity? What words should you use to carry on the parent/teacher conferences?

1. Take time to pray for the wisdom of the Holy Spirit. Don't respond to an e-mail or voicemail until you have talked to Jesus and maybe a colleague. (*James 1:5a "If any of you lack wisdom, let him ask of God,")*
2. Consider the situation, but understand that you cannot script your conversation because of the

uncertainty of a parent's thoughts and/or perspectives. *(Luke 21:14-15 "Settle it therefore in your hearts, not to meditate before what ye shall answer: For I will give you a mouth and wisdom, which all your adversaries shall not be able to gainsay nor resist.")*

3. Yield your personal struggle with the situation to Christ Jesus. Humble yourself before the Lord and let him be your judge. *(James 4:7 "Submit yourselves therefore to God. Resist the devil, and he will flee from you.")*
4. Allow the Spirit to talk in and through you with grace and truth. (*Matthew 10:19-20 "...take no thought how or what ye shall speak: for it shall be given you in that same hour what ye shall speak. For it is not ye that speak, but the Spirit of your Father which speaketh in you.")*

Giving Christ the control of my heart and tongue before meeting or communicating with my parents has proven to be a best practice. Over the years, the Spirit has given me wisdom and the exact words to speak that I could never have planned. An odd comment made by my principal after a tough conference comes to mind, "You are the only teacher who I have seen make a strong onion taste sweet." I can humbly say that they were not my sweet words but the Spirit of my Father in me. I praise Him!

"How sweet are thy words unto my taste! yea, sweeter than honey to my mouth!" Psalm 119:103

Dear Heavenly Father,

Thank You for caring about every detail of my life. Forgive me for fretting and a bad attitude. I submit this parent to You and ask You to put the appropriate words in my mouth. May she be assured that I love her child. Give me Your words. In Jesus' name, Amen.

Bible Reading – Psalm 37:1-11

NOTES

____

____

____

____

____

____

____

Classroom Practices

Respond with Purpose

"Let your speech be always with grace, seasoned with salt, that ye may know how ye ought to answer every man."

Colossians 4:6

Hallway conversations with students can happen for a lot of different reasons. Just being called to the hallway can cause apprehension and possibly frustration for students. Whether negative or positive, a teacher's part in each dialogue should be purposeful and with a tender heart. Trust and relationships can be built by the way we speak and interact with our students.

The best teacher of all, Jesus, used the following strategies in His conversation with the woman at the well in Chapter 4 of John:

1. **Listen** – Jesus allowed the Samaritan woman to speak and ask questions without interruption. *Allow students to talk as you listen.

2. **Sidestep & Redirect** – The woman was surprised that Jesus, a Jew, would speak to her a Samaritan. Culturally that was taboo. That was not the issue at hand, so Jesus redirected the conversation with truth – he would give her living water. He never addressed the inflammatory racial issue. (vs. 9 & 10) *If a student brings up racial bias, redirect to discuss the matter at hand.
3. **Don't Debate** – The woman pointed out that Jesus didn't have anything to draw water with and asked if he was greater than Jacob. She recognized that Jesus hadn't come to the well prepared and surely was not as important as Jacob, the Jewish patriarch. Jesus was greater than Jacob, but he hadn't come to the well to convince the woman of his credibility. He was there to meet her need of eternal life with living water. He redirected the conversation to address His purpose. (vs. 11 – 14) *Don't allow a student to provoke you into an argument. Return to the purpose of the conversation and remain calm.
4. **Grace with Truth** – Jesus knew all about the woman. When he told her to call for her husband, she said she didn't have a husband. That was true, but she was not innocent. Jesus accepted her response as truth but added that she had been married five other times. (vs. 16-18) *Many

times a student will lie or share partial truths. Affirm the truth he shared and show grace in how you respond.

In that short dialogue at the well, a relationship started because Jesus was purposeful in His conversation. The woman was no longer worried about the cultural differences or comparing Jesus to someone (Jacob) that she had trusted in for years. She believed and took Jesus as her Savior which in turn affected her community.

We can't provide eternal life, but we can create positive relationships by having honest purposeful conversations with our students by following Christ's example.

"A word fitly spoken is like apples of gold in pictures of silver." Psalm 25:11

Dear Lord Jesus,

Thank You for Your living example from the Word of God. Your ministry on Earth was not without challenges and yet You were always purposeful in each word that You used. Meeting the specific needs of those You ministered was always at the forefront of Your mind. As I interact with my students today, may I remember the example that You set before me and follow in Your footsteps. I choose to build relationships and make a difference in my students' lives for Your honor and glory. In Jesus name, Amen.

Bible Reading – John 4

NOTES

Classroom Practices
Extinguish Anger

"A soft answer turneth away wrath: but grievous words stir up anger."

Proverbs 15:1

I walked into the school office and heard screaming and profanity in the main conference room. It was out of control. I could see the frustration on my principal's face as he approached me outside that room.

He said, "You had his brother last year. How did you handle his anger? Dad is in there right now and things have gotten worse."

I explained that there was only one time when his brother started to scream and cuss at me. Without raising my voice, I told him to have a seat and calm down because I wouldn't listen to anyone who acted that way. "I don't talk to you that way," I said, "I'll be over in a little bit to listen to you."

I explained to the principal that once the student calmed down, he cried and apologized to me. He told me that he and his parents yell and cuss at each other at home when they are mad, so his cussing just came out with his frustration. I don't think that helped my principal in that moment, but that child's story is true for too many of our students. These Biblical principles should help us to extinguish anger:

1. Take care of your own attitude – (Colossians 3:8) - *Don't address the situation when you are angry. Stop, breathe with prayer, and then respond.*
2. Set a good example – (Titus 2:7) – *Walk in a godly manner to model good responses to tough situations.*
3. Be slow to anger & show understanding – (Proverbs 14:29) – *Be proactive not reactive. Be discerning of situations that may trigger anger in a child.*
4. Don't argue to perpetuate the anger – Proverbs 15:18 – *Keep your composure and calm even if provoked. Choose words that will guide the child where you want him to be with his behavior and/or learning.*

As you can see, our attitude is often the controlling factor. The Spirit is with us so keeping our heart in tune with God and His ways are key.

"Let your speech be always with grace, seasoned with salt, that ye may know how ye ought to answer every man." Colossians 4:6

Dear Lord Jesus,

Thank You for Your forgiveness and eternal love. Forgive me for allowing others to control my attitude. Help me to be like You in all my actions today. I ask You to calm those who struggle and help me to be discerning enough to prevent volatile situations. Empower me to know how to deal with those who struggle. In Your name, Amen.

Bible Reading – Colossians 3

NOTES

Classroom Practices

No Response Necessary

"Whoso keepeth his mouth and his tongue keepeth his soul from troubles."

Proverbs 21:23

It was the worst year of my teaching career. Students were mean to each other and unresponsive to any attempts that I made to change that. They were disrespectful to me and to each other multiple times each day. I found myself to be a lot more negative than positive most days. To improve my approach of handling the students' behaviors I spoke to the assistant principal more times than I like to admit. He came into my class to chat with my students on more than one occasion with no improvement. For the first time in twenty-three years, our LEAD officer walked out of a classroom for their disrespect and misbehavior. That was my class!

Parents were not supportive and usually found a way to blame me or another student for their child's behavior. The worst e-mail that I have ever received was a three-paragraph rant accusing me of being a bully and a copy of Indiana Code which defines bullying. I sat and cried. I was ashamed and felt condemned. (I'm not a bully! I love my students.) Since it seemed to be a legal threat, I asked my principal to read it and advise me. Needless to say, she was appalled and upset for me. She wanted to contact that parent and set him straight on my behalf. I just wanted her to know in case someone should contact her. "Please don't tell anyone about this," I cried.

After praying and asking the Lord to search me and forgive me for any wrongdoing, I confessed that I loved my students and wanted to respond in a godly way. I asked for the Lord's guidance. Should I tell anyone else? (no) Did the recipient ask any questions that needed answered? (no) Will a response make a difference? (no) I was reminded that Jesus had nothing to say about the false accusations against him before his crucifixion. I found peace with no response. Thankfully, I never heard from that parent again. That threat was squelched by my Heavenly Father. Praise His name!

"Therefore the prudent shall keep silence in that time; for it is an evil time. Seek good, and not evil, that ye may live:" Amos 5:13-14a

Dear Lord Jesus,

Thank You for continuing to work on me and for Your forgiveness. I know that I have not handled all classroom situations perfectly and have allowed my attitude to be swayed by students' behaviors. I choose to emulate Your kindness and love to my students, parents, and colleagues. I refuse to accept false accusations and choose to live my life to please You above all else. Guide in the way that I respond to any communication with my parents. I strive to be more like You and to be a light in this dark world. Thank You, Lord Jesus! Amen.

Bible Reading – Mark 15:1-5

NOTES

CLASSROOM PRACTICES
STICKS AND STONES

"For in many things we offend all. If any man offend not in word, the same is a perfect man..."

James 3:2a

"That was dumb!" said one student to another whose head dropped immediately.

"Don't talk like that," I corrected.

"He's my friend. He knows I wasn't trying to hurt his feelings," he responded, as he patted his buddy on the shoulder.

"That's unkind. Do you like to be called dumb?" I asked both boys.

The insulted boy said, "No," and walked away.

Unfortunately, that interaction between the buddies is not an uncommon way for people to talk to each other. Sarcasm and unchecked words flow freely from our mouths without considering how our words affect others. I can't count the number of times that I remind my students, "If you don't have anything nice to say, then don't say it at all." I believe that is a biblical principle which is nicely stated in Proverbs 10:19; "..he that refraineth his lips is wise."

In my morning circle, I shared a story that my dad taught me: A person came to a minister to apologize for gossiping and using unkind words. The wise clergyman took the gentleman to the church belfry with a down pillow. He ripped it open and let all the feathers float to the ground. He looked at the man and said, "Now, go gather all of those feathers and bring them back and completely stuff this pillow."

The man was perplexed, "That can't be done."

"I don't doubt your sincerity, but the words that you have spoken can never be taken back, not even with an apology," the pastor reproved. Words can be more harmful than sticks and stones, contrary to the adage, so choose them wisely.

When working closely with other staff members, I choose that "the words of my mouth be acceptable" in the sight of the Lord, as David wrote in Psalms 19:14. Throughout the Proverbs we are encouraged to use pleasant words. When we answer someone, it should be with "soft words." We set the tone of our relationships by the words that we use and how we speak those words. Even, tough conversations will be accepted by our colleagues more readily if we are thoughtful and deliberate with our words. Our words are powerful! Let's allow the Spirit to guide in what we say.

"Let no corrupt communication proceed out of your mouth, but that which is good to the use of edifying, that it may minister grace unto the hearers." Ephesians 4:29

Dear Heavenly Father,

Thank You for providing guidelines for how to speak to each other in Your Word. Help me to choose my words wisely before allowing them to flow freely. I choose to think before I speak and to only speak when it is acceptable to You. I yield my thoughts and feelings afresh to You. Help me, Lord! In Jesus' name, Amen.

Bible Reading – Psalm 19

NOTES

Classroom Practices
You Dare Not Touch Me

"Finally, my brethren, be strong in the Lord, and in the power of his might."

Ephesians 6:10

It was an eventful day in the library. I entered a little before dismissal and spotted one of my students running in anger toward another student. I got the student's attention and told him to stop. His anger then turned toward me with his fist clinched and cocked back, he aggressively came toward me. I pointed my finger at him, and his eyes met my eyes as I strongly warned, "You dare not touch me!" He stopped in his tracks and came no closer. It was as if his arm melted by his side.

My good friend, the librarian, was in awe. Later she shared in amazement how shocked she was that he stopped immediately and wondered what I would have done if he had hit me. I praise the Lord that I didn't have to physically protect myself. God's power in that moment was more appreciated and evident to me later in the year when the young man was suspended and didn't return for weeks because of his violent tendencies and threats. Knives were removed from his home and other possible tools that could be used as weapons locked behind doors so his brother and family would be safe.

I believe that the armor of the Lord and the words I spoke in the power of Jesus were what stopped the boy's attack on me. Being purposeful about putting the armor of the Lord on every day is essential. Our fight is a spiritual fight as believers, and we must not forget that. Unfortunately, Satan uses anybody and anything to destroy us. If a child is troubled and susceptible to the spirit world, he can be a conduit for the work of the devil. As I pray for each student in my classroom, I bind any works of darkness that may challenge me or destroy my class. I take the armor of God and hold on to His Word. I am more than a conqueror. (Romans 8:37) I praise the Lord that we can walk in His power and might. (Ephesians 6:10) Gird up and be strong!

"... he that is begotten of God keepeth himself, and that wicked one toucheth him not." 1 John 5:18b

Dear Heavenly Father,

Thank You that the same power that raised Jesus from the dead dwells within me. I choose to walk in Your Spirit today as I minister to my students. I bind any wickedness that would hinder me or my class today. I put on the shield of faith, the breastplate of righteousness, the helmet of salvation, and the entire armor of God. Thank You for keeping me safe and secure today. In Jesus' name, Amen.

Bible Reading – Ephesians 6:10 - 17

NOTES

Section 4 – Rely on Him

Rely on Him

Jesus Cares

"...I will never leave thee,
nor forsake thee."

Hebrews 12:5b

The Lord will not give us more than we can bear.
He gives us promises that His Word doth declare.

When our trials and burdens seem quite unfair,
He gives us friends with which we can share.

Even when we are mad and would not dare,
He wants us to come to Him with every care.

He loves us and never wants us to fear.
He wants us to realize that He is ever near.

The Son gave His life to make it real clear
That He loves and cherishes each of us dear.

So go to the Master with all your affairs,
He's listening and waiting to show you He cares.

Dru Pearcy

"Casting all your care upon him; for he careth for you." 1 Peter 5:7

Dear Lord Jesus,

Thank You for reminding me that You care. Things are tough right now, and it gives me great peace to know that You love me. I'm lonely right now, but I know You are near. Your Word is a comfort to me so help me not to be consumed by the circumstances around me. Thank You for hearing my prayers even through my tears. I love You! Amen.

Bible Reading – 1 Peter 5

NOTES

Rely on Him

Teacher Needed

"Give instruction to a wise man, and he will be yet wiser: teach a just man, and he will increase in learning."

Proverbs 9:9

For the past few years, assessments seem to be more stressful than ever for students. Whether a pre- or post-test students seem to need reassurance that all is fine. "Is this test for a grade?" inevitably is asked.

Whether it is for a grade or not, I tell them that their assessments will help me know what I need to teach them. "I would not expect you to get a perfect score on this pre-test. If you already know it all, then you wouldn't need me as your teacher." That seems to calm most of the students, however, there are a few who are still overwhelmed with the thought of failure.

None of us like to fail or struggle. We strive for perfection and frequently fall short. Circumstances can cause us to struggle and can be quite baffling at times.

Job, an upright and a God-fearing man, endured unbelievable loss and suffering. Twelve times "teach" was used in the book of Job. He was a just man, but there were still lessons to be learned.

The matured disciples were never without need of their Teacher. In Mark 6, Jesus empowered them to heal and cast out demons. They were successful in healing and delivering those with great needs. However, in Mark 9, the disciples seemed powerless to help a sick, demon possessed son. After Jesus healed and delivered the son, the disciples asked what they could have done differently. Their failure led to another lesson to be learned from Jesus, the greatest teacher of all times.

Job and the disciples experienced significant successes but not without failures, trials, and temptations. If they had had a life of perfection, they wouldn't have needed the Teacher. There were lessons to be learned. Just as I want my students to realize their need for me as their teacher, we must not forget the need of our Teacher. There is more to be learned!

"Teach me good judgment and knowledge:" Psalm 119:66a

Dear Lord Jesus,

Thank You for being my lifetime teacher. Forgive me when I forget that one reason for my struggles is to learn one more lesson from You. Help me to gain good judgment and knowledge from Your Word and to rely fully on You to teach me. Thank You for Christian colleagues that help me along the way. In Your name, Amen.

Bible Reading – Mark 9:20-30

NOTES

Rely on Him

God Knows

"O LORD, thou hast searched me, and known me. Thou knowest my downsitting and mine uprising, thou understandest my thought afar off."

Psalm 139:1-2

Recently, teachers were given access to an APP that monitors student computer activity. From home, our desk, or anyplace in the building, we can check students' activities while they are at school. We want our students to be safe online and to use the appropriate programs for our lessons. We can lock and/or send a message to the students who are off task without saying a word. It is an effective way to keep students accountable and to make them aware that we know what they are doing.

This year on more than one occasion, a Christian colleague shared with me how God had spoken to her through a song as she traveled to work. She came in at the end of one day with joy to share that she heard the same song three times that day. "God must be trying to get my attention," she says with a smile, "He knows!" On other occasions, she has shared how the words and examples that I have used during our Bible time have the same messages as she heard from her pastor.

During our last Bible time, our small group listened as my friend shared that her needs were met one more time by a Christian song on her way to school. It is amazing how God knows exactly what we need. Her teammate pointed out, "It's just like (our new app)." We can see what our students are doing and try to guide them with prompting. Likewise, God does the same. God sees and knows, too!

"For the ways of man are before the eyes of the Lord, and he pondereth all his goings." Proverbs 5:21

Dear Heavenly Father,

Thank You for knowing exactly what I need. Whether it's a verse of scripture, a song, words from a friend, or a message from the pastor, I choose to acknowledge Your presence in my life. Help me to listen and stay on task to fulfill Your will in my life. As

I teach today, help me to be discerning and to walk in Your Spirit. In Jesus' name, Amen.

Bible Reading – Psalm 139

NOTES

Rely on Him

Eyes in the Back of His Head

"The eyes of the LORD are in every place, beholding the evil and the good."

Proverbs 15:3

One boy whispered to another, "How did she see that? I clicked it off before she could see it."

"She has eyes in the back of her head and sees everything," teased his buddy.

"How did you know? How did you see what he was doing?" he asked.

"Just a watchful eye," I grinned in response.

Truthfully, there are many things that get past me. I do not see all things, nor does any other teacher. Unlike us, our Heavenly Father sees all things. He sees the good and the bad. Nothing gets by Him!

When we disobey the Word of God or have selfish intentions, God sees and judges us by His Word. He convicts and calls us to repent (change our ways). Unfortunately, in some areas of our lives that may be a daily battle just like some of us experience with our students. Thankfully, God sees and is merciful.

When we live righteously, God sees and will reward us accordingly. Satan would have us believe that our righteousness is not seen. At times, we may feel like the quiet, well-behaved student who gets overlooked. As teachers, we may not acknowledge that student as often as we should, but God is not slack. There is comfort in knowing that He sees our faithfulness and righteousness. In God's own timing and way, the righteous will be rewarded either here on Earth or in Heaven. He is faithful!

Job was a righteous man who went through terrible hardships. God allowed Satan to take his possessions, his family, and even his health. But, God never took His eyes off Job. God restored his health, wealth, and family in God-like fashion: exceedingly abundantly above all that he could even imagine. (Ephesians 3:20) God never takes His eyes off us either.

"He withdraweth not his eyes from the righteous:" Job 36:7a

Dear Heavenly Father,

Thank You for being my all-seeing Father and knowing my every move. Help me listen to the conviction of the Spirit and seek Your forgiveness when I am wrong. I choose to be faithful and righteous in Your eyes. I know that my troubles are a means for You to draw me nearer to You. I find great comfort in knowing that You never take Your eyes off me or those that I love. I trust You! In Jesus' name, Amen.

Bible Reading – Psalm 33

NOTES

Rely on Him
Clinging

"I will not let thee go, except thou bless me...and he blessed him there."

Gen. 32:26, 29

It was a rough morning for one of my students. When she returned to me from her morning class, she was a mess. My teaching partner explained that the young lady refused to do any work for her, so she would need to stay in with me for recess to work. I decided to have the little one stay with me for lunch and recess. I asked her what was going on that she didn't do her work. That is when the floodgates opened. She was bawling. I couldn't hear what she was saying, so I had her come to my desk. Sobbing, she reached out for a hug. I extended my arms and that is when both of her arms wrapped around my neck and her face went into my shoulder. I held and rocked her until she calmed down enough to tell me of her hurt. My shoulder was wet from her tears. She hung on tight until she received the comfort that she needed.

Being able to nurture and comfort students is one part of a teacher's calling. Too often the needs of our students are far greater than we can meet. We can be overwhelmed and come to doubt ourselves. Tears flow when we realize our insufficiency to do it all. Our clinging should be around the neck of Christ Jesus by holding tightly to His will and trusting the promises of His Word. When Jacob (Gen. 32) held on to his antagonist, he was in an exhausted state. He had no other energy than to hang on until the blessing came. We must stop wrestling with what is going on with our classroom children, family, health, job, and rest with our arms around the Master. If our hands are clinging to our own solutions and ideas, we cannot cling with a full grasp to what God has for us. Cling! Hold on! Don't let go of Christ and His promises!

"I cling to you; your right hand upholds me." Psalm 63:8 (NIV)

Dear Heavenly Father,

I feel overwhelmed with all that is going on right now. I ask You to forgive me for trying to figure it all out on my own. I choose to cling tightly around Your neck and hang on to Your promises. You promised never to leave me. I believe! I thank You for all things because I know that You have a plan that needs to be fulfilled. I'm trusting You this day. In Jesus' name, Amen.

Bible Reading – Genesis 32:24-30

NOTES

Rely on Him
Step on It

"He maketh my feet like hinds' feet: and setteth me upon my high places."

2 Samuel 22:34

I was drowning! As a fourth-grade teacher, I had a class of 33 students. I dealt with physical pain for months. We had new teaching strategies that we were required to use. We had to develop and execute a new intervention system with students who were struggling. We had a new reading curricula and hands-on science kits to put together and use. Assistants in and out of my room created a whole different stress. The rigor and expectations were overwhelming.

I vividly remember a chat I had with our literacy coach one morning. She asked how I was doing. "My nose is barely above the water. I'm drowning!" I confided in her. She asked me if I had ever heard of the folktale, "The Donkey and the Farmer." She went on to explain that the donkey got stuck in a well and was too heavy for the farmer to rescue. The farmer called for his neighbors to come and help him bury the donkey because he was just too far gone to be rescued. The farmers all began shoveling dirt into the well. Before long, something unexpected happened. The donkey stepped out of the well! He had used the very dirt which was burying him to step on and walk up out of his predicament. She encouraged me to step on the strategies, new curricula, new intervention expectations, all the responsibilities, and breathe. I took her advice and looked at each challenge as a steppingstone to make me a better teacher for Jesus' sake.

Praying, trusting in the Lord, and relying on Him each step of the way has been the key to enduring tough expectations and trials of life. Although the requirements, twists and turns of education, and stresses of meeting individual needs can be taxing, we can exalt our Heavenly Father as David did in 2 Samuel 22. David endured much and was able to see God in and through the difficult events of his life. He acknowledged God's hand in and through it all by giving Him thanks.

"Thou hast enlarged my steps under me, so that my feet did not slip." 2 Samuel 22:37

Dear Heavenly Father,

Thank You for always getting me through the difficulties of life. Help me to keep my eyes on You when I feel that I am drowning. I choose to step on and live above the circumstances for Your honor and glory. I lean on You to give me strength to successfully fulfill Your plan for my life. I love You and choose to please You, In Jesus' name I pray, Amen.

Bible Reading – 2 Samuel 22

NOTES

Rely on Him

God Is Bigger

"…because greater is he that is in you, than he that is in the world."

1 John 4:4b

Mental health has become a focus lately. Teachers and students alike are looking for peace and a way to cope with school and personal lives. Many circumstances are beyond our control, but peace for a believer comes by knowing God is BIGGER than any problem. We must not sway from believing the truth that there is nothing impossible for Christ Jesus. "If God be for us who can be against us?" (Romans 8:31b) When we have the Creator God with us, it doesn't matter what comes our way. He is over all!

As I think about the bigness of God and His unfathomable power, I am awestruck! In many cases, He spoke, and it came to pass. During the six days of creation with each and every detail of its grandeur, it came into being just by the Creator God saying, "Let there be...," (Genesis 1) and each and every time it came into being. In the New Testament when the disciples' ship was threatened by the storm Jesus said, "Peace be still," (Mark 4:39) and the sea became calm. The disciples said, "Even the winds and the sea obey him." (Matthew 8:27) There is case after case in Jesus' ministry on earth that He showed His compassion and spoke miracles into being. He healed, delivered, and raised people from the dead. Some may say that we cannot expect the same from Him today. However, the Bible tell us that Jesus is the same yesterday, today, and forever. (Hebrews 13:8) If God did miracles before Christ walked on earth, and Jesus performed miracles while here on earth, then the Spirit of God will and can be revealed through miracles today, too. When looking into the storm of life, I can confidently say, "My God is BIGGER." John stated in his gospel, "My Father … is greater than all." (John 10:29)

God's ultimate power was displayed when he raised Jesus from the dead. Satan could not hold him in the sealed tomb. Think about this! Our risen Savior by the Holy Spirit indwells every believer. That is breathtaking, and a truth that we need to hold onto as we face conflicts of this life. We can fully rely on and trust in the power of Christ Jesus. Miracles still happen to bring honor and glory to the Heavenly Father and to bring men and women to Christ Jesus. Ultimately our God is Sovereign and what he says will come to pass. No matter your struggle, find your peace in knowing that God is BIGGER!

"Nay, in all these things we are more than conquerors through him that loved us." Romans 8:37

Dear Heavenly Father,

My heart is burdened today, but I find great peace in Your bigness. I'm grateful that when there doesn't appear to be hope, that Your Word and works encourage me. I know that I am victorious because the same power that raised Jesus from the dead dwells in me. Thank you, Jesus, Amen.

Bible Reading – John 10:23-30

NOTES

____

____

____

____

____

____

____

Rely on Him

Giants

"...and the Lord is with us: fear them not."

Numbers 14:9b

One of my students upon receiving the unit assessment immediately became exasperated. He teared up, pushed the packet to the side of his desk, and proceeded to tell me that it was too long and too hard for him to do. The apparent size of the task overwhelmed him before he even looked at the questions. At that moment, it was his giant.

What giant are you facing today? Are you overwhelmed and fearful? Are you doubtful of God's love and hand in the matter? Can you see past the circumstance to draw strength from our Almighty God? There are two specific accounts in the Bible that I am thinking of today that dealt with giants. One ended in defeat, the other in victory.

Spies were sent by Moses to survey the land promised by God. There were giants in that land and ten out of twelve of the spies could only think and talk about the size of the warriors. Although they found and brought the people huge, delicious clusters of grapes, pomegranates, and figs, they focused on the size of the giants. Joshua and Caleb, two God-trusting spies, reminded the people that the Lord was with them, so they had nothing to fear. God's goodness and promises were completely ignored due to their focus, the giants. The Israelites wept and allowed fear and anger to grip their hearts. Defeated and without hope, many lost their claim to the Promised Land.

Later in Israel's history, the army of Israel was challenged by a Philistine giant. Goliath taunted the Israelites daily for forty days. His size and constant threat caused the army to tremble. It wasn't until a shepherd boy arrived in camp that courage was displayed. David heard the giant blaspheme the Lord and by faith took courage to fight him. He saw the giant just like his brothers and army, but he found power in knowing God had delivered him before and would do it again. He proclaimed to Goliath, "This day will the Lord deliver thee into mine hand;..." (1 Samuel 17:46) David's smooth stone was guided by Almighty God and the apparent invincible foe was defeated. Victory was won because David put his trust in God who is over all giants!

We all face giants. Human nature would have us run, be afraid, allow stress to control, and/or be filled with despair when facing our own giant. Faith would have us cling to God's promises and in what the He has prepared for us. God is for us and with us. Don't be afraid!

"The Lord is on my side; I will not fear: what can man do unto me?" Psalm 118:6

Dear Heavenly Father,

Thank You for promises that I can hang on to. Forgive me when I focus on the giants all around rather than You, my Mighty God. Encourage my friends to trust in You. Embrace them and remind them of Your promise to always be with them. I claim victory for me and them today. In Jesus' name, Amen.

Bible Reading – Numbers 13:25 – 14:9

NOTES

____

____

____

____

____

____

____

Rely on Him

Exceeding Abundantly Above All

"Now unto him that is able to do exceeding abundantly above all that we ask or think, according to the power that worketh in us,"

Ephesians 3:20

There is power in word choice. Students become better writers when they include adjectives, adverbs, and use powerful verbs. Paul could have said "…is able to do all that we ask…," but he chose three descriptors, "exceeding abundantly above," which extend and highlight the true power of God. He emphasizes the possibilities with God which are beyond our comprehension. We have a Savior who performed countless miracles while here on Earth and proved Himself faithful. We may struggle with doubt, but He remains faithful.

Building our faith scripture upon scripture is essential. Connecting Bible passages to each other is like using conjunctions in grammar. For, and, nor, but, or, yet, and so are small words that connect and help to build further thought from a writer. Conjunctions were used in each of the following verses and connect to the truth that Paul so strongly emphasized about the exceeding power of our Living Savior. (Bolded words were added by me.)

1. "And Jesus looking upon them saith, With men it is impossible, but not with God: **for** with God all things are possible**."** **Mark 10:27**
2. "**And** whatsoever ye shall ask in my name, that will I do, that the Father may be glorified in the Son." **John 14:13**
3. "But as it is written, Eye hath not seen, **nor** ear heard, neither have entered into the heart of man, the things which God hath prepared for them that love him." **1 Corinthians 2:9**
4. "But Jesus beheld them, and said unto them, With men this is impossible; **but** with God all things are possible." **Matthew 19:26**
5. "Believe me that I am in the Father, and the Father in me: **or** else believe me for the very works' sake." **John 14:11**
6. "If we believe not, **yet** he abideth faithful: he cannot deny himself." **2 Timothy 2:13**
7. "**So** then faith cometh by hearing, and hearing by the word of God." **Romans 8:17**

"And this is the confidence that we have in him, that, if we ask any thing according to his will, he heareth us:" 1 John 5:14

Dear Heavenly Father,

Thank You for being God who answers above and beyond what we ask or think. There are so many needs, and some seem impossible. Help my unbelief. I trust Your Word and lean hard on You today. Nothing is impossible for You, so if it be your will please heal, deliver, and provide a way for victory for Your name's sake. Amen.

Bible Reading – Ephesians 3:7-21

Notes

____

____

____

____

____

____

RELY ON HIM

FIVE LOAVES AND TWO FISHES

"And they did eat, and were filled: and there was taken up of fragments that remained to them twelve baskets."

Luke 9:17

As I read this morning from Luke chapter nine, I came across a very familiar story but need to apply it a bit differently in my life today. The people were hungry and had need. The disciples didn't have enough to meet the needs of the 5,000 people. They wanted to send them back to town for lodging and food. Jesus said, "Give ye them to eat." The disciples said, "We have no more than five loaves and two fishes." (Luke 9:13) Jesus had them organize the group into fifties to prepare them to eat. He took the five loaves and two fishes, which are all that the disciples had to offer, and looked up to Heaven, he blessed them, and brake, and gave them to the disciples to feed the 5,000. Not only were they all fed but they had twelve baskets leftover.

Realistically, we are all limited in and of ourselves. I have said often as others in my profession, "I'm doing all that I can. I can only do so much." In essence, that is what the disciples were saying.

Think about the amount of food they had to offer: one loaf per 1,000 people and 2/5 of a fish per 1,000 people. Jesus had the disciples organize the people to prepare them to receive the food. As I teach, I need to prepare my students to receive what God has for them. Notice, I did not say what I have to offer them. I don't have enough for all the needs of my students. However, I can certainly trust my Heavenly Father to bless what I have to give. He can take my limited resources and multiply them. He can give my students an understanding of what I must teach. That in no way relieves me of the responsibility of using my God-given gift to teach, but it forces me to wholeheartedly rely upon God to increase my resources and meet the needs of each child in my classroom. If God chooses and it's His will, He can multiply the limitations of me and my students. That is my prayer today!

"And what is the exceeding greatness of his power to us-ward who believe, according to the working of his mighty power," Ephesians 1:19

Dear Lord Jesus,

Forgive me for stressing over the "what ifs" of this life. There are many stresses in this life, and I find myself with many limitations. Where I fall short in resources, I ask You to multiply them a thousandfold today. Give me the knowledge to know how to teach my students, the strategies that will work to meet their learning styles, and the resolve to always reflect your love and kindness to each child. I commit my students to you and ask that You bless and multiply the offerings that I present each day. May there be baskets full of knowledge, understanding, and values leftover for my students to take on in this life. I thank You that You care about what is going on in my world. I thank You for Your promises and I claim Your rewards and blessing for me and my students today. Amen

Bible Reading – Luke 9:10-17

Notes

Rely on Him

Backpacks Too Heavy

"Come unto me, all ye that labour and are heavy laden, and I will give you rest."

Matthew 11:28

One of my students was struggling to pick up her backpack. I leaned over to help her pick it up and was quite shocked by how heavy it was. She was quite petite and carrying a bag that was half her weight. I offered to help her carry it, but she said, "I've got it. I carry it all of the time." I suggested that she leave some of the things in her locker, but she insisted upon carrying everything around with her.

A story that I heard years ago was brought to remembrance. A farmer was traveling down a dirt path in his wagon when he saw a stranger walking and bent under a load. As he drew closer, he called to the man and offered him a ride. The farmer offered his hand and pulled the stranger up next to him. With the heavy knapsack on his shoulder, he sat next to the farmer. After they traveled a distance, the stranger complained of his shoulders and back hurting. The farmer said, "There's no need to carry that load. There's plenty of room in the wagon. Toss your knapsack back there." It wasn't until the stranger tossed his knapsack into the wagon that he was relieved of his burden.

We often allow the needs of our students, pressure of school expectations, and our personal struggles to burden us down. We think we must be strong and tend to carry the load on our own. Jesus invites us to come to Him with all our problems, and He will give us relief. Until we toss or cast all those needs, cares, and struggles on Christ, we will be overwhelmed and continue to hurt. God is holding us in His hands and wants us to allow Him to fulfill all our needs. Take off that heavy backpack of care and cast all your heaviness onto Christ Jesus, the One who cares for you deeply.

"Casting all your care upon him; for he careth for you."
1 Peter 5:7

Dear Heavenly Father,

Thank You for caring so deeply for me, my students, and my loved ones. Forgive me for trying to carry my own burdens and not releasing them to You. I cast all my cares afresh on You today. When I become overwhelmed, remind me of Your precious promise of rest and peace. I choose Your peace that passes all earthly understanding. In Jesus' name, Amen.

Bible Reading – Psalm 55:16-23

NOTES

RELY ON HIM

MOUNTAIN BE GONE

"... for verily I say unto you, If ye have faith as a grain of mustard seed, ye shall say unto this mountain, Remove hence to yonder place; and it shall remove; and nothing shall be impossible unto you."

Matthew 17:20b

Struggles are real for all of us. Oftentimes, our colleagues know very little about the challenges that we face outside of the classroom. Our finances, family relationships, and health needs are all things that consume our minds. When facing my challenges, I must admit that one moment I am convinced and believe with my whole heart that my burden is an ant hill as I view it from God's point of view. The next minute, I am looking up and can't see past that elevated mountain of circumstances. It is my reality and circumstances of life that Satan tries to use to control and threaten me. There is no denying when there is a huge problem.

Regardless of the expected outcome, I say by faith unto the mountain of circumstance; "Be removed into the sea! I refuse to doubt the power of my omnipotent Creator God."

All that God requires of me is to have the faith the size of a mustard seed. A mustard seed is no larger than 1 or 2mm and very difficult to see if held as a single seed in between two fingers. I confess that I have at least that much faith, so when Satan tries to convince me otherwise, I will not listen to him. I will continue to claim the victory. For nothing is impossible with Christ Jesus. (Luke 1:37) He is my miracle working Savior!

In Matthew 17, Jesus told the disciples if they had the faith of the grain of mustard seed and would SAY unto the mountain to be removed to another place that it would be removed…and NOTHING shall be impossible to them. Jesus also informed them that their challenge would only be solved by prayer and fasting. That indicates that some effort in spiritual warfare with prayer and fasting may be necessary for such difficult things to be removed. We need to say and pray to get results. Not only am I to pray for God's hand in the situation but to claim with the words of my mouth that it shall be even as I say, according to God's Word. Above all my desires and words of faith, may God's will be done!

"Jesus said unto him, If thou canst believe, all things are possible to him that believeth. ... Lord, I believe; help thou mine unbelief." Mark 9:23-24b

Dear Heavenly Father,

Thank You for the Word of God which feeds my faith. I am overwhelmed with burdens. Forgive me for my lack of faith. I know that I have at least faith the size of a mustard seed, therefore, I hope in You. I choose to use my words to praise You and to claim all that You have for me and my family. Whatever happens, I accept Your will and only Your will for me. In Jesus' name, Amen.

Bible Reading – Matthew 17:14-20

Notes

____

____

____

____

____

____

Rely on Him

Peace, Be Still

"Thou wilt keep him in perfect peace, whose mind is stayed on thee: because he trusteth in thee."

Isaiah 26:3

A dear colleague confided in me that her husband had cancer, and the prognosis was not good. Another teacher came to my room after school in tears, "I need your prayers. My family is falling apart." On another occasion, a young teacher came to me sobbing. She had lost her baby. Heartbreak and personal storms are inevitable. Peace comes when we trust in the Master of the Storm, Christ Jesus.

The storm was raging! The wind was fierce, and the ship was filling up with water quickly. Jesus was sound asleep. How could He sleep through the entire clamor, the rocking, and all the turmoil on that ship? The disciples were frantically trying to keep the ship from sinking as the Savior was sound asleep. They did all that they could do to keep the ship from taking on water. Fear set in and they felt certain they were going to sink. They had to wake Jesus. The disciples questioned Him and wondered if He even cared. Jesus stood up and rebuked the wind and said unto the sea, "Peace, be still." (Mark 4:39) The swirling storm ceased and there was a great calm. Jesus then questioned the disciples' faith. Why did they allow fear to rule their thinking? Understandably, the storm was intense and one that could have possibly taken their lives. The conditions did not look good at all, but Jesus was with them. Jesus was concerned about their lack of trust and faith in Him. They should have trusted and rested in Him.

Too often we are looking at the twenty-foot swells of induced stress and hardships that engulf our life and falter in our faith. Faith allows us to experience calm as the winds and storms are swirling about us. Peace comes by knowing that Jesus has not left us, because He promised. We will not be exempt from trials and tribulations, so we must hold to the truth that Jesus has already overcome anything that comes our way. The key to that statement is that "Jesus has overcome" so our hope is in Him. Instead of looking at the swells of this life our mind must stay on the Comforter, who is the Master of the Storm. "Peace, be still," (Mark 4:39) was enough to calm the storms then, and it is enough to calm the storms of life today.

"... but be of good cheer; I have overcome the world." John 16:33b

Dear Lord Jesus,

Save me! I'm drowning! Increase my faith and help me cling to your Word. Forgive me for looking at the overwhelming circumstances. I claim peace through Your Word and choose joy. Thank you for never leaving me. I trust You right now. In Your name, Amen.

Bible Reading – Mark 4:35-41

NOTES

Section 5 –
Pray & Pray More

Pray & Pray More

I'm Going to Tell Jesus on You

"Rejoicing in hope; patient in tribulation; continuing instant in prayer;"

Romans 12:12

Your lack of motivation is disheartening!
What more can I do or say to help you succeed?
I'm going to tell Jesus on you!

Your antics and defiance drive me nuts!
Nothing I say seems to change your behavior.
I'm going to tell Jesus on you!

Your anger and personal attacks are hurtful!
No matter how nice I try to be, you are mean.
I'm going to tell Jesus on you!

Your disengagement and sadness trouble me.
How much more should I know about you?
I'm going to tell Jesus on you!

You are a delight and a blessing to me.
How can I make your school year better?
I'm going to tell Jesus on you!

"I'm going to tell Jesus on you," came from an elderly lady in my uncle's church. She cared deeply for others and wanted them to know she was praying for them. I try to make a practice of praying for my classroom students each morning on my way to school. Jesus has the answers and will give me discernment on how to care for each child. I choose to rejoice, be patient, and continue to pray for them all! I don't hesitate to tell Jesus about my students because He loves them even more than I do.

"But Jesus said, Suffer little children, and forbid them not, to come unto me: for of such is the kingdom of heaven." Matthew 19:14

Dear Heavenly Father,

Thank You for the ministry of teaching children. Forgive me when I allow the poor attitude of students to control my attitude. I choose to bring each student to You daily in prayer. I lean on You to give me discernment on how to minister to every child that You have placed in my care. Thank You for hearing and answering my prayers. In Jesus' name, Amen.

Bible Reading – Matthew 18:1-11

NOTES

Pray & Pray More

Needle in a Haystack

"But the very hairs of your head are all numbered. Fear ye not therefore, ye are of more value than many sparrows."

Matthew 10:30-31

I sat down at my desk after dismissal and realized that my small 1.5 inch by 3/8-inch thumb drive was missing. I searched my desk, the floor, the trash can, and then I had a panic attack. That drive had all my schoolwork, our church information, along with my husband's business financial reports. I asked teachers if they had seen it. I went to the office and spoke with the assistant principal about the possibility of it being stolen by a student. I had allowed a student to sit at my desk and use my computer. With no proof, how should I handle this situation? After getting back to my classroom, I sent out some texts and asked for prayer. As I drove home, tears flowed as I prayed for the Lord to intervene. I didn't sleep well that night, so I prayed more. The next morning, I asked my students if anyone had seen it or picked it up by accident. I didn't get a response and moved on. Every spare moment I prayed. Before the end of the second day, I saw the red light on the phone was lit up. A stranger left me his phone number and said that he had found my thumb drive. I called him immediately. The gentleman explained that he found the drive in the mulch under the swing of their neighborhood playground. He had been swinging his two-year-old daughter and noticed a small shiny object. (The guy had enough technological experience to use my thumb drive to figure out that it was mine and even where I teach.) I set up an appointment to pick up the thumb drive the next day.

I had to tell others. On the way to the office, I let my teacher friends know. I told the whole amazing story to the assistant principal. "That's unbelievable. That tiny little object was found in mulch and then someone was able to locate you."

With goosebumps, I said, "That's a miracle!"

God answered my prayers. He reminded me once again that He cares about every little or big detail of my life. That tiny, little thumb drive was important to me. He knew exactly where it was from the time it left my desk, how it was thrown away in the mulch, and placed that young father in the playground to find it. With every new and challenging situation, I must remember to rely on God. After all, He has my hairs numbered and He sees and knows all about me just like when a bird falls from the sky. My thumb drive was like a needle in a haystack, and He restored it to me. Be encouraged! Great or small trust that God sees, hears, and cares for you, too! Trust in Him!

"For the eyes of the Lord are over the righteous, and his ears are open unto their prayers…" 1 Peter 12a

Dear Heavenly Father,

I cannot praise You enough for hearing and answering my prayers. I know that You see and care about every detail of my life and classroom. That brings me peace. May You be glorified today. In Jesus' name, Amen.

Bible Reading – Matthew 6:25-34

NOTES

____

____

____

____

____

Pray & Pray More

He Shut the Lion's Mouth

"Ye shall not fear them: for the Lord your God he shall fight for you."

Deuteronomy 3:22

One day after taking students to art class, my principal was waiting for me in my classroom. I could tell that he was worried which was unlike him. He explained that one of our parents was threatening to call the local TV station and sue the school. The disgruntled mother had already called the superintendent and was demanding a meeting. Apparently, Mom felt that her child's IEP was not being followed by my team of teachers, and she was going to let the world know. To meet the parent's demands, my principal set the appointment up for the next afternoon. I hadn't done anything wrong, and the accusations against my teammates were unfounded. This irrational momma bear was out for blood, and her threat was intimidating.

I set out to pray and pray and pray. Words would not be enough to reason with our upset parent. She was determined that someone would pay for what she perceived as incompetency. I was reminded of the story of Daniel. The presidents and princes set out to get rid of Daniel, a righteous man. His habit of praying three times a day landed him in the lion's den. God shut the lion's mouth, and Daniel was unscathed. If God could do that for Daniel, He could do it for me! I specifically prayed and asked the Lord to shut down the mother's irrational threats of bringing the media and suing us. God answered my prayer!

When we met, there were no TV cameras and no mention of a lawsuit. The sweet mother was rational and just wanted what was best for her child. With kindness, my teammates and I were able to convince her that we cared deeply for her child and the things that needed addressed would be. After the meeting, my principal and teammates looked at each in amazement. "That is not the same woman that I spoke to yesterday," said my principal with relief. God shut the lion's mouth that day! To Him be all glory!

"Fear thou not; for I am with thee: be not dismayed; for I am thy God: I will strengthen thee; yea, I will help thee; ..." Isaiah 41:10a

Dear Heavenly Father,

Thank You for being my Almighty God! I do not want to assume that just like many angry parents this one will calm down too. I know that ultimately You are in control of everything in my life because I surrender to You. I trust You to deliver me and my team today from this terrible threat on our careers. I believe as You closed the lions' mouths for Daniel that You will do the same for me today. Thank You for caring about every detail in my life. In Jesus' precious name I pray, Amen.

Bible Reading – Daniel 16

NOTES

Pray & Pray More

Plus Prayer

"...who is even at the right hand of God, who also maketh intercession for us."

Romans 8:34b

"What does impact mean?" asked a student as we began an assessment.

"Really?" I thought. For six straight days, I went over the focus question. We defined, gave synonyms, and ended each lesson with something that pointed to how the culture had an impact on the characters in the first few chapters. We had read, discussed in partners and whole group, took notes, and debriefed as a class, and there were still students that did not get it. Considering how Christ taught and the disciples learned, perhaps, I should have prayed more!

In John 17, Jesus tells of his teaching and the disciples' learning:

1. Introduce the topic with repetition – (vs. 5-6) "I have manifested thy name…" Jesus introduced the Heavenly Father to those following Him. He told of the Heavenly Father before the beginning of the world six times in John 1. Ten times in the Book of John, Jesus emphasized the Father that sent Him. *Building background knowledge is essential and repeating important information is necessary for understanding.*
2. Take notes – (vs. 6) "…and they have kept thy word." In the Old Testament the Children of Israel were told to write the law on door posts and keep them in view and in their mind. *That would be like notetaking today.*
3. Understanding – (vs. 7-8) "Now they have known that all things whatsoever thou hast given me are of thee….; and they have received them." *Students have enough understanding to have conversations and answer questions.*
4. Apply – (vs. 8b) "…and they have believed that thou didst send me." One of the Greek definitions for believed is "to be persuaded of." *When students can use what they have learned they will write about the topic.*
5. Pray for them – (vs. 9) "I pray for them:" Jesus told the Heavenly Father of the disciples spiritual

learning then prayed for them and us. *Our students need our continual prayer.*

Let us examine our knowledge, understanding, and application of the Word of God. As teachers we may get frustrated with students but imagine how Jesus feels when we don't seek knowledge, grasp His Word, or walk in the Spirit. He is patient and prays for us. Let us follow His example and pray for our students too.

"Examine yourselves, whether ye be in the faith; prove your own selves..." 2 Corinthians 13:5a

Dear Heavenly Father,

Thank You for being patient when I am not in tune with You. Forgive me when I don't seek You as I should. Give me a clearer understanding of the things that You have prepared for me. Help me to be as diligent in praying for my students as I am about teaching them. May I always pray for them as You pray for me. In Jesus' name, Amen.

Bible Reading – John 17:1-9

NOTES

PRAY & PRAY MORE

FLEECE OF CONFIRMATION

"The eyes of your understanding being enlightened; that ye may know what is the hope of his calling, and what the riches of the glory of his inheritance in the saints,"

Ephesians 1:18

I was on the corporation discussions committee for years. Our leader was moving out of state. I was honored to be asked to be her successor. Should I, or shouldn't I take the lead? On another occasion, the principal offered me a position on the school improvement committee. Should I, or shouldn't I? Many opportunities are available if we are interested. Leadership roles usually lead to career advancements which can be good. However, those roles can be stressful and cause us to be too busy to give our time to God. It is important to pray and ask for signs at times, before making decisions, especially those of great commitment.

God called Gideon to lead the Israelites. He was a farmer, a common man, who had very little confidence in himself. He needed God to convince him that he was truly the one to save Israel out of the enemy's hand. Gideon set out a fleece of wool not once but twice. He insisted upon God showing him definite signs. The first evening he wanted the dew to only be on the fleece while the grounds around it stay dry. It happened just that way! However, just like most of us that was not enough for Gideon to believe that God wanted him to lead the Israelites. He apologetically asked God to prove Himself once more but this time by keeping the fleece of wool dry while the ground around it was wet with dew. It was just as Gideon had asked! Finally, he was convinced of God that he was the chosen one. Have you ever questioned whether it is God's will for you to do or have a certain thing? Seeking clarity and asking God as Gideon did for something specifically may be what He wants from you.

Gideon's dilemma was in confirming God's will for his life. I have struggled at times in the same way and have found that as I seek the Word of God and follow God's ways, the Holy Spirit leads and answers the prayers that I offer. Sometimes He even provides a sign of confirmation if I ask. He can do the same for you as you seek His guidance.

"Ask, and it shall be given you; seek, and ye shall find; knock, and it shall be opened unto you:" Matthew 7:7

Dear Heavenly Father,

Thank You for leading and guiding in my decisions. I choose to seek You in all my choices. Show me in Your Word what You would have me to do. Thank You for the leadership opportunities that I have been given. I draw strength and discernment from You today. In Jesus' name, Amen.

Bible Reading – Judges 6:11-40

Notes

Pray & Pray More

Hailstones and Sunshine

"If God be for us, who can be against us?"

Romans 8:31b

Just like most teachers in Indiana, I gave myself to intense prayer for my students' success on the state assessment. As I read my Bible, I was encouraged by an unlikely passage. As crazy as it may seem, as my students were taking their test, I was claiming "hailstones and sunshine" for them. I asked God to bring hailstones to defeat all fear and lack of confidence. I claimed God's sunshine to give them a clear, sound mind as they took the test. My prayer was that their enlightened minds would perform well for the sake of Christ and for His glory.

In Joshua 10, God promised the Israelites to deliver their enemy into their hand. With God on their side, the Israelites snuck up on the enemy who then fled in fear. As the enemy scattered and ran, God sent hailstones from heaven to destroy them! The Bible says, "...they were more which died with hailstones than they whom the children of Israel slew with the sword." (vs. 11) The victory was God's!

To finish that battle, Joshua spoke to God and asked that the sun stand still. They needed more daylight time to annihilate the enemy. Think about that request! Who could make the sun stand still? God! Joshua asked and God provided. The scripture says, "And the sun stood still, … for the LORD fought for Israel." (Joshua 10:13)

If the Lord fought for Israel, He will fight for us. The devil tries to destroy our credibility, our reputation, and our testimony in any way that he can. State assessments have brought teachers' undue stress. They are used to evaluate students, teachers, schools, and school districts. The threat of failure is present. Yet some are facing far more serious issues: such as poor health, broken relationships, addictions, family difficulties, financial struggles, and some are grieving over a loved one. God knows each struggle and will guide us to victory as we yield to His ways.

Regardless of what we are facing, hailstones and sunshine from our Almighty God are there for our taking. When the Israelites obeyed the voice of God and allowed Him to fight for them, there was always victory. On that one sunshiny day in history, God used hailstones and sunshine to defeat the enemy. I have found great hope and courage by claiming hailstones and sunshine on more than one occasion! Allow Christ to fight for you today!

"For God hath not given us the spirit of fear; but of power, and of love, and of a sound mind." 2 Timothy 1:7

Dear Lord Jesus,

Thank You for providing examples of Your grace and victory throughout the Bible. I choose to allow You to fight my fight today. I trust You to send hailstones to crush my fears and any threats against me. I claim sunshine to provide clarity in the decisions that I make. I know that my victory is Your victory, so I trust You fully today. In your precious name I pray, Amen.

Bible Reading – Joshua 10: 1-14

NOTES

____

____

____

____

____

____

Pray & Pray More

Pray for Your Leader

"Continue in prayer, and watch in the same with thanksgiving;"

Colossians 4:2

One morning during our school prayer time, one of the secretaries shared with me that our new principal was irritated with me. I asked, "Why? Did I say or do something to offend her?"

"It upsets her when you tell her that you are praying for her," she explained.

"Oh my! Maybe I need to explain. When I say I'm praying for her, it is not to be critical but to lift her up to the Father who can meet all her needs. I've often said I would not have a principal's job."

A principal carries a heavy load. There are many things that we cannot do for those around us, but our Father in Heaven can meet those needs. The best thing I can do in those types of situations is to pray. Once my principal came to know me better, she knew that I wasn't being critical of her but supportive. From time to time, she would say that she could use my prayers. She knew I cared because I prayed.

When Queen Esther needed to approach the king, she faced the possibility of death. She needed courage to enter the king's presence, and it would take God to change the king's heart about the dire situation. The queen sent a message to her uncle and her Jewish people to fast and pray. She was praying but understood the importance of having others praying with and for her. When the time came, God gave Esther the courage, softened the king's heart, and delivered her and her people. By praying and fasting the people were an essential part of Queen Esther's success. Her success preserved their lives, too.

Our administrators need our prayers. Pray that they have the courage and discernment to make hard decisions. Ask the Lord to give them wisdom and concise words to speak when called upon. Pray faithfully for God's hand and blessing. When they are successful, we will be.

"Ask, and it shall be given you; seek, and ye shall find; knock, and it shall be opened unto you:" Matthew 7:7

Dear Heavenly Father,

Thank You for blessing me with wonderful administrators. I count it a privilege to work with them. Today, as they make hard decisions, give them wisdom and understanding to make good choices for Your name's sake. Strengthen and encourage them in each conversation and circumstance that challenges them. Help them to seek you for all things. I trust You to guide them as they guide me and our staff members. In Jesus' name I pray, Amen.

Bible Reading – 1 Timothy 2:1-8

NOTES

____

____

____

____

____

____

____

Pray & Pray More

God Prays for Us

"... he maketh intercession for the saints according to the will of God."

Romans 8:27b

Finding a small group of believers to pray and fellowship with has been a strength to me for the past few years. Meeting weekly with a thought, devotion, scripture, and prayer together has been a blessing. Knowing that my fellow teachers are praying for me means so much. From time to time, a good friend has taken time to pray with and for me. Requesting a prayer through text, e-mail, or in the hallway is not uncommon. We support each other in prayer. That support at times is my lifeline, but there are times that I feel that I need more than their prayers. I need someone who is bigger!

We have someone more powerful that is making intercession and praying for us to the Father. It is Jesus Christ! Think of that! Before Jesus was crucified, he prayed to the Father for His disciples and then went on to say that He is praying for us who come to believe on Him. I am a believer, so Jesus is praying for me. Romans tells us that He searches our hearts and knows the mind of the Spirit. When He prays, Christ knows the Father's will for us and can pray in that fashion. God hears Him and those prayers are answered. Too often as teacher friends we come short in knowing how or what to pray for each other. Knowing that colleagues are praying is an encouragement but even better is knowing that Jesus is praying for us in every area of our life and for our ministry of teaching. What a comfort!

"Neither pray I for these alone, but for them also which shall believe on me through their word." John 17:20

Dear Lord Jesus,

Thank You for giving me friends and family that pray faithfully for me. More than them, I praise You for making intercession on my behalf and praying for the precise things that I need in my life. You know more than I do of what it is that I am missing. I trust You to fulfill Your will in my life, as I seek Your ways. I uplift my friends to You and believe You will minister to them today. Be glorified in all my ways. In Your name I pray, Amen.

Bible Reading – John 17:9-26

Notes

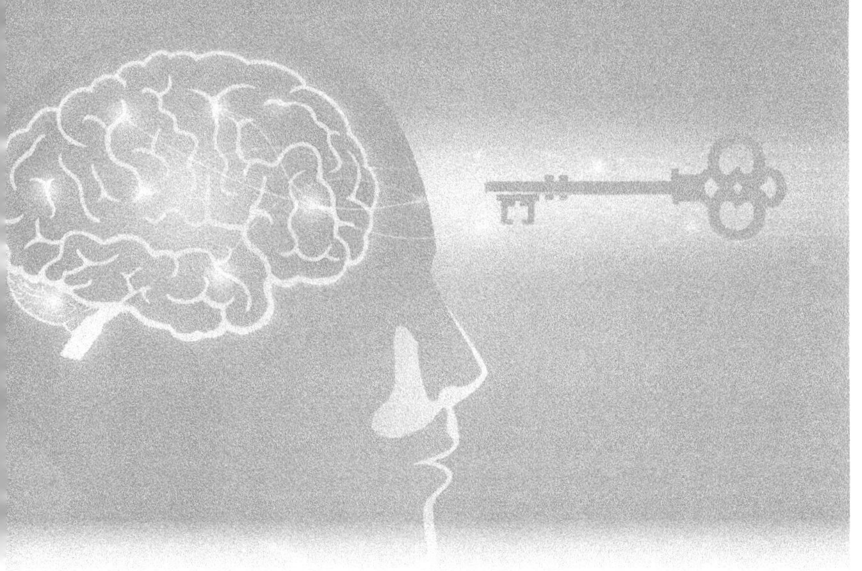

Section 6 – Mindset is Key

Mindset Is Key

My Identity

"(For we walk by faith, not by sight:)"

2 Corinthians 5:7

A good friend reminded me in prayer that my disappointments do not define my identity. My identity comes through Christ Jesus and what His Word has to say about me, not necessarily what I think of myself or what someone else may think of me. I wear many hats as a Christian, and I am eternally grateful for who Christ through the Holy Spirit has made me. When I am down, I remind myself of what God says about me in His Word. He truly defines my identity by His grace and mercy.

I am loved by the Lord Jesus. – John 3:16, John 15:9

I am a child of the King. – John 1:12

I am begotten of God and the wicked one touches me not. – I John 5:18

I am more than a conqueror. – Romans 8:37

I am an heir and joint heir with Christ Jesus. – Romans 8:17

I am justified and glorified in Christ Jesus. – Romans 8:30

I am a vessel unto honor and sanctified. – II Timothy 2:21

I am forgiven. – I John 1:9

I am His sheep. – Psalms 23, John 10

I am a friend to Jesus. – John 15:14-15

I am a servant of Christ. – Psalms 134:1

I am not condemned. – Romans 8:1

I am represented by my advocate the Heavenly Father. – I John 2:1

I am a soldier of the Lord. – Ephesians 6:12-17

I am an ambassador of Christ Jesus – II Corinthians 5:20

I am a saint. – Romans 1:7

I am in the eternal race. – I Corinthians 9:24

I am a tree of righteousness. – Isaiah 61:3

I am a royal priesthood. – I Peter 2:9

I claim my spiritual identity in Christ Jesus and believe it fully by faith! I remember a statement that my dad had in his pastoral office. It said, "Believe it in your heart. Say it with your mouth. For you have what you say!" Solomon in Proverbs warns us not to be snared by the words of our mouth. When negative words proceed from my mouth, they are a snare to my spiritual being. We must speak God's Word in belief and walk in freedom. Know who you are in Christ Jesus!

Thou art snared with the words of thy mouth, thou art taken with the words of thy mouth. Proverbs 6:2

Dear Heavenly Father,

Thank You for the Word of God and its truth. Forgive me for growing discouraged. I claim my identity in You and refuse to allow negative words to trap me. Thank You for the encouragement of Your Word and promise.

I am who You say that I am! In Jesus' name I pray, Amen.

Bible Reading – John 14

NOTES

Mindset Is Key

I Am Okay

"And she said, It shall be well ... And she answered, It is well:"

2 Kings 4:23b & 26b

Passing in the hallway one teacher asks, "How are you today?"

"I'm okay," I respond.

"Are you sure? You look like something may be troubling you," questions my friend.

"I'm hanging in there," I assure her as I continue walking.

There is a lot going on and my heart is troubled, but after my morning time in devotion and prayer I choose to trust in Jesus. When I say, "I'm okay," or "I'm hanging in there," that is my proclamation of faith that with Christ all will be okay. The trouble still exists, but I choose to be confident in God's love for me. If I'm overwhelmed when saying "I'm okay," I call upon a teacher friend to pray with and for me. That prayer of faith then boosts me to say, "It's all good!"

I've been encouraged by the faith of a woman in Elisha's time in 2 Kings 4. Tragedy struck when her son died. She was determined to find the man of God. As the donkey was being prepared, the woman had a conversation with her husband and said, "It shall be well." (vs. 23) Her son was dead and yet her faith said, "It will be okay." The mother's faith must have grown as she got closer to her destination. When asked by Elisha's servant if everything was well with her, her husband, and son, her response was one of faith, "It is well." (vs. 26)

The woman's son was still dead, and yet that was her response. She could say that because she knew who to go to for answers. It was to God through the man of God. The woman wasn't without tears and questions when she was hanging on to the feet of Elisha, but she kept her hope in God's goodness and grace. The mother stayed with Elisha until her son was raised from the dead. Ultimately, there was rejoicing, and literally it was well with the child.

As I spend time with Jesus and allow His Word to minister to me, then I truthful can say, "I'm okay," for I know that nothing is impossible for Him!

"...If ye have faith as a grain of mustard seed...nothing shall be impossible unto you." Matthew 17:20

Dear Lord Jesus,

Help me to be honest about the affairs of my life first with You. I choose not to be in denial of my problems but wholeheartedly choose to trust in You, my Almighty God. When I need help and prayer from others, help me to swallow my pride and ask. I'm grateful for the truth that nothing is impossible for You, and though my faith be small, You will make a way. In Jesus name, Amen.

Bible Reading – 2 Kings 4:14-37

NOTES

____

____

____

____

____

____

Mindset Is Key

MINDSET

"The purposes of a person's heart are deep waters, but one who has the insight draws them out."

Proverbs 20:5 (NIV)

At the beginning of the school year our class talks about fixed mindset versus growth mind set. We go over different scenarios and discuss how we can change our mindset for growth. As opportunities arise throughout the year, I try to help students change their mindsets. A mindset of faith is important to us as believers.

In Daniel 3, there is an account of three men's faith and mindset: Shadrach, Meshach, and Abednego. In vs. 17, "..., our God whom we serve <u>is able to deliver</u> us from the fiery furnace, <u>and he will deliver us</u> out of thine hand, O king." (underlined words added for emphasis) Wow! What words of faith and trust in God for deliverance! The mindset of the men is shown in the next verse, when they said, "But if not,.." (vs. 18)

They would not bow even if God chose not to deliver them. Instead, the faithful men made a commitment to God by their confession to the king and faced the fiery furnace. Their faith and mindset were essential. Faith says, "God will do this." Mindset says, "If He doesn't, I will only worship and obey Him."

Thirty years ago, I faced a pivotal point in my faith and mindset. My mom was dying of cancer. I wrestled with three small words from scripture; "But if not,..." What if it wasn't the way I wanted it? I prayed and believed God could heal her. But if not, was I going to serve the Lord and be okay with what He deemed best? After a few days of tears and turmoil, my mindset had become if God didn't heal my mom, I would fully trust and serve Him. I continued to pray for healing but ended each prayer with "not my will but thine be done." It was painful to lose my mom, but I felt the presence of God then and now because I set my mind to love Him and serve Him no matter what.

What is your mindset? Do you believe God loves you and is able to answer your heart's desire? Will you praise Him and serve Him regardless of the outcome of your hardship? Just as the Son of Man was with the men in the fiery furnace (vs. 25), He is with us. No matter the difficulty, have faith in the Savior and allow your mindset to be adjusted by the Word of God. Choose Him above all else!

"...choose you this day whom ye will serve; ...but as for me and my house, we will serve the LORD." Joshua 24:15

Dear Heavenly Father,

Thank You for Your presence in my life, especially during hardships. They have been painful, yet they have brought growth to my faith. I believe in miracles and hope to see them, but I also know that You have divine purpose for me and my loved ones. Regardless of outcomes, I cling to You. In Jesus' name, Amen.

Bible Reading – Daniel 3

NOTES

____

____

____

____

____

____

____

Mindset Is Key
Talk Positively to Yourself

"... he shall have whatsoever he saith."

Mark 11:23b

Mental health is a huge focus in our schools and for good reason. Recently, our administrators and counselors set out to encourage staff members by sending daily e-mails with self-care activities. One week, the strategies were centered on taking five minutes for self and to think on positive things. Thinking positively is good, but sometimes the negative thoughts make it difficult. Talking to ourselves with Biblical passages and principles can help us overcome.

Philippians 4:8 reminds me to think on the positive things not on the negative. When I think of the goodness of the Lord, I overcome and get back on track mentally. Then I can be a blessing to others. Clichés and empty words do very little to change a person's negative mindset. However, the Word of the Lord gives life to those who will grasp hold of it.

When things seem too bad or the absolute worst, remember God is good! It's not just a cliché! Say, "God is good! He is above all that is against me. I trust in His goodness now and refuse to doubt Him." Quote the following passage/s.

"Praise ye the Lord. O give thanks unto the Lord; for he is good: for his mercy endureth for ever." Psalm 106:1 (Psalm 107:1; Psalm 118:1; Psalm 118:29; Psalm 136:1)

When you are overwhelmed with worry and fear, let the peace of God rule in your hearts. Say, "Thank you Lord for peace that passes all understanding. (Philippians 4:7) I will not worry because you are the God of all comfort. I claim peace today."

"And let the peace of God rule in your hearts,…and be ye thankful." Colossians 3:15

When things seem out of control, God has us in His hand. Say, "I am in my Father's hand and praise Him for protecting and shielding me from all harm. This circumstance will not consume me because the Master holds me tight."

"My Father, which gave them me, is greater than all; and no man is able to pluck them out of my Father's hand." John 10:29

When I feel alone or like others are against me, I remember God is for me! Say, "Thank you Lord for being on my side. I am above this attack because you are for me. I am victorious!

"...If God be for us, who can be against us?" Romans 8:31b

"And ye shall know the truth, and the truth will make you free." John 8:32

Dear Heavenly Father,

Thank You for the Word of God and its truths. Thank You for being so good to me. My peace comes by knowing that You are above all else and You have me in the palm of Your hand. Help me to remember my identity, according to Your Word. In Jesus' name, Amen.

Write your praise down, thank Him in prayer, or tell others of His blessings.

Bible Reading – Philippians 4

NOTES

____

____

____

____

____

____

Mindset Is Key

Panic Attack

"Be strong and of a good courage, fear not, nor be afraid of them: for the LORD thy God, he it is that doth go with thee; he will not fail thee, nor forsake thee."

Deuteronomy 31:6

It was test day! Students around the room showed signs of anxiety. One girl teared-up, a boy crossed his arms and slid down in his seat, and another student came to my desk immediately for help. Surprisingly, about halfway into the test a normally calm student came to my desk and told me that she didn't think she could do it. I could see the anguish in her face. She didn't want to fail. I told her it might help to take a break, so she went into the hallway. About ten minutes later my teaching assistant told me that she had taken the young lady to the counselor because she was sobbing uncontrollably. The next morning the student said, "I'm sorry about what happened yesterday. I have anxiety. It's been a long time since I have had an anxiety attack like that."

No one is exempt from anxiety. We all face challenges, wrestle with the what ifs of life, wait for unanswered prayers, and may feel threatened at times. From Genesis through Revelation, there are imperatives that address our human tendencies to worry and fret: Don't be afraid. Be strong. Be courageous. Don't worry. Don't fret about it. Don't be anxious. Be encouraged, I am with you. Those are short and to the point. We can deal with our fears and anxieties without having a panic attack when we place our faith in God's Word of hope.

Just like my student, our anxiety goes undetected by others until we are confronted head-on with a challenge. My student successfully implemented coping skills for testing after her panic attack. To extinguish panic attacks, God has given us His Word to cope with any issue with strength and courage. It is up to us to implement His Word for success. Find some verses, memorize them, write them down, put them where you can readily see them. Allow God's Word to bring you comfort and victory over any anxiety that you may face. A panic attack is imminent without it.

"The Lord is on my side; I will not fear: what can man do unto me?" Psalm 118:6

Dear Heavenly Father,

Thank You for being in control of all circumstances. When my heart drops because of pressures and fears, I trust Your promises. You are with me. Help me not to allow challenges or the unknowns to overcome me. I know You are on my side, and I trust You to work things out right now. In Jesus' name, Amen

Bible Reading – Deuteronomy 31:1-8

NOTES

Mindset Is Key

I Thought

"For my thoughts are not your thoughts, neither are your ways my ways, saith the Lord."

Isaiah 55:8

We teach our students to be problem solvers which is a good life skill. However, sometimes our problem solving may interfere with God's planned solution. As intelligent people we often think we know what should happen in specific circumstances or how God should work things out in our lives. Unfortunately, our thoughts can be irrelevant if they don't align with God's plan for us.

Naaman was a Syrian captain who had leprosy. He heard of the prophet, Elisha, who had the ability to heal him. So, Naaman traveled with his horses and chariot expecting to be greeted by Elisha, but instead, Elisha sent his servant to tell Naaman to go wash in the Jordan River seven times in order to be cured. It infuriated

Naaman. In 2 Kings 5:11, it says, "But Naaman was wroth, and went away, and said, Behold, *I thought*, (added italics) He will surely come out to me, and stand, and call on the name of the Lord his God, and strike his hand over the place, and recover the leper." Naaman envisioned the steps of his healing differently. He thought...but it didn't happen that way!

The Jordan River was also known as the "muddy river" and the river itself was not the cure. Being obedient to the instructions of the man of God was necessary for the healing of the leper. There was nothing hard about dipping in the river seven times. That was the problem! Naaman had expected something more difficult or some magical hand-waving prayer by Elisha. It angered Naaman because it wasn't as he thought it would be. With the persuasion of his servants, however, Naaman dipped in the Jordan seven times and was healed.

How many times do we become frustrated because our life is not like we thought it would be? I thought...... but it is not that way! We are looking for something or someone other than God to cure or solve our problems. Naaman's expectation of being healed was fulfilled, but it did not happen as he thought it would. Whether the solution is simple or difficult it doesn't have to be as we think as long as the Heavenly Father can be glorified. God calls us to obey, trust, and allow Him to solve our problems whatever they might be.

"Commit thy way unto the LORD; trust also in him; and he shall bring it to pass." Psalm 37:5

Dear Heavenly Father,

Thank You for being in control of my life. Forgive me for being frustrated when things don't go the way I think they should. I commit my situation to You and choose to follow the leading of the Spirit. I praise You for always working things out according to Your plan for me. In Jesus' name. Amen.

Bible Reading – 2 Kings 5:1-14

NOTES

____

____

____

____

____

____

____

Section 7 – Our Daily Walk

Our Daily Walk

Infinity

"As far as the east is from the west,
so far hath he removed our
transgressions from us."

Psalm 103:12

As I read a novel the other day, I was reminded of a few math lessons that I taught years ago. Counting to 100 was no big deal but counting to 1,000,000 was. We did not attempt it due to time. Practicing equations with numbers in the billions or trillions tended to give students a glimpse of the immensity of their value. To help students visualize infinity, I drew a line with arrows on the ends. "Numbers go on and on," I explained. Still, it was difficult for them to understand.

Just as it is hard for students to fathom a gazillion, eternal life is hard to grasp. By faith, we can grab hold of God's promise of the everlasting life spoken of in John 3: 16. "For God so loved the world, that he gave his only begotten Son, that whosoever believeth in him should not perish, but have everlasting life." Believing and receiving the truth that Jesus loved me so much that He died to take away my sins and become my Savior guarantees me eternity with Him. That means I will live with Him forever and forever and forever. Heavenly bliss will never end.

Excitedly, I look forward to being with Jesus one day, but sometimes Heaven seems so far away. While here, I find great joy in His infinite forgiveness. My salvation is secure, but I deal with sin daily. Satan, the accuser, wants me to feel guilty and condemned. Victory is mine because when I ask Him for forgiveness, I am eternally pardoned. How high is the sky? Where do east and west start and end? Infinite forgiveness has been promised to me now and an eternal home with Christ is mine by His grace. Confidence is mine because of His infinite love and eternal promises.

"For as the heaven is high above the earth, so great is his mercy toward them that fear him." Psalm 103:11

Dear Heavenly Father,

Thank You for giving Jesus to die for my sins. Thank You for forgiving and forgetting my transgressions. Your eternal promises provide me hope and peace. I choose to live a life pleasing to You and will share Your truth with others. Thank You for loving me. In Jesus' name, Amen.

Bible Reading – Psalm 103

NOTES

Our Daily Walk

Scoot Over to God's Side

"But it is good for me to draw near to God:..."

Psalm 73:28a

Have you ever felt all alone even though you are surrounded by supportive colleagues? Emotionally, that is not uncommon. When going through such a time, I reflect on all my relationships, especially my connection with God. Let's ponder these thoughts about God: How far is God from you? How close are you to God?

<u>How far is God from you?</u> God's distance never changes. He is where He has always been. He promised never to leave me nor forsake me. (Hebrews 13:5) God is with me always! If that is the case, then why do I still feel that He is a million miles away? At times, I can't seem to feel God's presence. My prayers don't seem to be answered, and my Bible and meditation time don't seem to be as meaningful.

How close are you to God? When I feel lonely and a distance between me and my lovely Savior, I know it is not a "God" problem, but it is a "me" problem. Since God never moves then I must take an active part in drawing near to Him. Perhaps an apology should be my first step. Then, I can determine how close I am to God by actively pursuing Him in my daily life and conversations with Him.

My dad used to share this analogy: Years ago, cars and trucks had bench seats. When couples would go on dates, the young lady would sit right next to the gentleman. As newlyweds they would continue to show their affection by sitting closely together. As children came along and time passed, the wife ended up over on the other side of the bench seat close to the passenger window. One day the woman looked at her husband gloomily and said, "I wish things were the way they used to be." The husband responded in love, "I want that too. I haven't moved. I've been here the whole time." Christ has not moved. He is the driver and has control of what is going on in our lives. He is waiting for you and me to move closer to Him so we can feel His loving embrace.

"Draw nigh to God, and he will draw nigh to you."
James 4:8a

I must move closer to Him!

Dear Heavenly Father,

Thank You for never moving and always being with me. Forgive me when I become indifferent and stagnant in my walk of faith. I choose to rekindle my passion and love for You daily by meditating upon the Word and having intimate conversations with You in prayer. Today, I am scooting across that bench seat and holding on tight to the love of my life! I love You because You first loved me. Thank You, Lord Jesus, Amen.

Bible Reading – James 4

NOTES

____

____

____

____

____

____

Our Daily Walk

Acknowledge God

"And that every tongue should confess that Jesus Christ is Lord, to the glory of God the Father."

Philippians 2:11

"No way! I would get in so much trouble," said one student to another.

"Oh, come on! It's no big deal!" Coerced the adventurous student.

"Nope, I'm not doing it," as he walked away from the peer pressure.

It's not easy to walk away! Joseph was tempted repeatedly by Potiphar's wife in Genesis 39. Joseph's acknowledgement of God prevented him from sinning. He said, "... how then can I do this great wickedness, and sin against God?" (vs. 9) He cared deeply about what God would think and ran. Joseph's life was not easy. There is no indication that he grew bitter against God. It seems that when given opportunity that he had he would give credit to God. Joseph acknowledged God for his interpretation of the butler and baker's dreams. After interpreting the dreams for Pharaoh, he emphasized that God was in control of the events of the coming famine. Because Joseph repeatedly referenced God, Pharaoh recognized that he was a man with the Spirit of God.

None of us are exempt from temptations or trials. Whether a peer or our own desires are driving us to do something displeasing to the Lord, let's be as Joseph and consider God first. How can we sin against Him? Run! When opportunities arise to use our talents for Him, let's testify of God's gifts and goodness. Give Him the glory and acknowledge Him whenever possible. Let's not be negligent. Just as Pharaoh, came to realize that the Spirit of God was on Joseph, our colleagues and parents should sense God's presence in our lives.

"Whosoever shall confess that Jesus is the Son of God, God dwelleth in him, and he in God." 1 John 4:15

Dear Heavenly Father,

Thank You for the Spirit of God who dwells in me. When temptations come my way, help me to remember You and be strong. I choose to acknowledge You and praise You before others. May others know that you live within me. In Jesus' name, Amen.

Bible Reading – Genesis 39: 1- 12

NOTES

Our Daily Walk

Last to be First

"... If any man desire to be first, the same shall be last of all, and servant of all."

Mark 9:35b

"Mrs. Pearcy, he cut me," tattled a student as we lined up to leave the classroom.

"It doesn't matter where we line up," the guilty student responded.

"Then, you will be okay to move to the back of the line. Right?" I asked. The student dropped his head and walked to the back of the line.

Most of us are like the student who cut the line. We want to be first or near the front. The ego tends to look for recognition and to be first. Throughout the Gospels, Jesus addressed this with the disciples. There was even a dispute among the disciples because James and John's mother asked Jesus if they could have the seats next to Him in Heaven. What a lofty thought to be seated right next to Jesus in Heaven!

Perhaps the disciples felt close enough to Jesus to ask for that position, however, Jesus knew their hearts. Pride was still present in their lives. Thinking of their own placement in Heaven, instead understanding what was about to happen to Jesus, showed their pride. Jesus reminded them that to be great among people, they must minister or serve them. He used His own life as an example and said that He didn't come for others to serve Him, but He came to serve them. A servant is a lowly position and quite humbling. The Word of God contradicts our earthly thinking. To be first we must be last and servant of all. (Mark 9:35) Servitude is part of God's design for our lives. Let's be Christlike and provide service with a smile.

"For I have given you an example, that ye should do as I have done to you." John 13:15

Dear Heavenly Father,

O, to be like Jesus is my desire. Forgive me where I have neglected to humbly serve others. I choose to understand Your ways, even though at times they aren't my ways. I humble myself today to serve and love others as opportunities arise. I choose to please You above all else. In Jesus' name, Amen.

Reading Text – Matthew 20:20-28

NOTES

Our Daily Walk

I Admire You

"When he shall come to be glorified in his saints, and to be admired in all them that believe..."

2 Thessalonians 1:10a

Recognizing one's value and worth is essential. "I admire you" is quite the compliment, especially when it comes from a beloved colleague and/or friend. Over the past couple of months, I have been blessed by such kind messages. The most recent, "I'm so blessed to know you, and I admire how you allow Jesus to shine through your life. I thanked God for our friendship today." I share the same admiration for her.

Admire is not a frequently used word so I decided to briefly research it. According to http://merriam-webster.com admire means "to feel respect and approval (someone or something): to regard with".[5] When I looked a little further, "regard" and "respect" have more to do with qualifications and considered evaluations over time. However, "admired" seemed, in my opinion, to suggest a more personal connection and understanding of the person being admired. Merriam-webster.com states, "ADMIRE suggests usually enthusiastic appreciation and often deep affection..." I propose that regard and respect are built upon over time; then with a personal relationship an admiration is developed with consistent positive patterns of personal and professional practices.

Mary, Martha, and Lazarus were siblings who befriended Jesus. They fed Him and spent time together. One verse tells us that Jesus loved them. (John 11:5) Apparently, they had become close friends because when Lazarus became deathly sick, Mary and Martha sent for Jesus. When Mary cried over Lazarus' death, Jesus wept. (John 11:35) He deeply cared. Mary knew Jesus' character and was blessed to witness His omnipotence when He raised her brother from the grave. When an opportunity came, Mary demonstrated her admiration for Jesus by anointing Him with her expensive

[5] "Admire." Merriam-Webster.com Dictionary, Merriam-Websster, https://www.merriam-webster.com/dictionary/admire. Accessed 19 July 2021.

perfume. Her extreme appreciation and deep affection were greatly appreciated by Jesus and were to be remembered. Admiration can be communicated in many ways. May we develop a relationship with Jesus that goes beyond basic respect and becomes a deep admiration that is witnessed by others.

"O magnify the LORD with me, and let us exalt his name together." Psalm 34:3

Dear Heavenly Father,

Thank You for your many blessings. Thank You for listening and answering my prayers. I choose to glorify You above everyone else. I choose to draw nearer to You and to be enthusiastic when expressing my admiration for You. May others magnify and exalt Your name with me. I love You! In Jesus' name, Amen.

Reading Text – John 12: 1-8

Notes

Our Daily Walk
Inward Beauty

"Favor is deceitful, and beauty is vain: but a woman that feareth the LORD, she shall be praised."

Proverbs 31:30

All girls want to be beautiful, and there are very few who believe they are. Just this week, I greeted one of my students, "Good morning, pretty lady."

She responded, "Are you talking to me?"

I said, "Yes, I'm talking to you."

I heard her mumble, "I don't look in the mirror and see that."

I reassured her, "You are beautiful!"

She did not consider herself to be beautiful. In fact, she would unlikely win a beauty contest, but she certainly is a beautiful person. I believe you must understand that God made you unique, and it is what He sees in you that matters anyway. Inward beauty comes in the form of our Godlike characteristics.

Proverbs 31 describes the Godlike characteristics that define true beauty. A beautiful person maintains a life of moral excellence. Her purity is marked by her walk of holiness. She is trustworthy and displays goodness instead of evil. She's a hard worker. A beautiful woman's strength and honor are observed by those around her. Her generosity and sympathy for those who are less fortunate are evident by her giving, and at times she sheds tears of compassion with and for them.

A beautiful person plans wisely. She is careful in her word choice and uses words of kindness to comfort others. A beautiful lady fears the Lord and obeys His commandments. She rejoices and has a face that shines like an angel. A mother's beauty is recognized by her children, and they praise her for her goodness.

Are you a beautiful person? Is your beauty only skin deep or is it far deeper? My concern is that girls young and old are trying to improve their outward beauty and are neglecting what truly makes them beautiful in God's eyes. It's the heart and spirit that He looks upon, according to I Peter 3:3-4, "... a meek and quiet spirit, which is in the sight of God of great price." It's what God sees that matters most, and your Godlike traits will be recognized by others as your true beauty.

"...the Lord seeth not as man seeth; for man looketh on the outward appearance, but the Lord looketh on the heart." I Samuel 16:7b

Dear Heavenly Father,

Forgive me for comparing my outward beauty to those around me. I thank You for making me unique. When I don't feel pretty, remind me of Your beauty standards. I choose to focus more on my inward beauty and exemplify godliness for Your name's sake. In Jesus' name, Amen.

Reading Text – Proverbs 31

NOTES

____

____

____

____

____

____

____

Our Daily Walk

A Resemblance

"But we all, …, are changed into the same image from glory to glory, even as by the Spirit of the Lord."

2 Corinthians 3:18

"I'm not Alyssa, Mrs. Pearcy. I'm Brooklyn," my student corrected me.

"Oh my! I did it again! I told you that you look just like Alyssa did in fifth grade. Not only do you look like her, but you have the same sweet disposition. That's a compliment to both of you." I apologized as I explained myself. I caught myself calling her Alyssa quite often.

Who do you look like? I can't count the number of times that I was told how much I looked like my dad. A few months before my dad died, tears came to his eyes, and he told me that I looked so much like my mom. I don't think I look like Mom, but he saw her actions and words in the things that I did for him. Not only do I look like my parents, but at times I have their same mannerisms and say the things they used to say. The more we are around a person, the more we think and act like them.

What would happen if we spent more time with Jesus? Many around us are thirsting for a true glimpse of a Christian who reflects the image of Jesus Christ. We must know Him personally to be genuine in our Christian walk. We need to know His character to live it. Before we can reflect Christ's image, we must spend time in devotion and in the Word of God to be able to emulate His character. Then we find ourselves speaking like Him and acting like Him. Remember, Christ Jesus was loving, compassionate, sacrificial, merciful, forgiving, patient, and longsuffering. Christians should manifest the fruits of the Spirit as Paul addressed in the book of Galatians. We may not have Christ's physical traits but without doubt we should have His spiritual attributes.

In Acts 4 after Jesus had ascended to Heaven, the people proclaimed that the disciples had been with Jesus. They recognized their resemblance to Christ Jesus by their speech and actions. The disciples displayed compassion and presented a message of repentance and hope just as Christ had in His ministry. What do our words and actions tell others? Do we resemble Christ enough for them to recognize us a Christian?

"...to be conformed to the image of his Son,..." Romans 8:29b

Dear Heavenly Father,

Thank You for being my Savior of hope. Forgive me when I fall short in my words and actions. I choose to know You better and to live a life that resembles Your life on Earth. As I resemble my godly parents, may I reflect Your image for others to be drawn to You. Be honored today. In Jesus' name, Amen.

Reading Text – Galatians 5:16-26

NOTES

____

____

____

____

____

____

____

Our Daily Walk

The Ripple Effect

"For none of us lives to himself, and no one dies to himself."

Romans 14:7

One pebble in the pond
A splash that makes more ripples
So many lives touched
Whether one thinks so or not
We all make a difference.

Ordinary rock
In an ordinary pond
The ripple effect
Positive or negative
It's a choice. Be a blessing!

Live above reproach.
Making ripples for Christ's sake
Positively live
Pleasing the Father foremost
Others reap the benefits

What you do matters
Your life intertwines with mine.
Lives entwine with you
Your pond with arms is open
Jump in! Make a good ripple.

"... but be thou an example of the believers, in word, in conversation, in charity, in spirit, in faith, in purity." 1 Timothy 4:12b

Dear Lord Jesus,

Thank You for making me a pebble in a pond of students and fellow teachers. You are my Rock and influence my life in all ways. Help me to create positive ripples for others to experience Your love. As my students move on, help them to create positive ripples of their own. I choose to be a godly example and to approach Your ministry for me with zest and will allow You to do the rest! Thank You for those who have touched my life with their ripples. Bless them. In Your precious name I pray, Amen.

Reading Text – Proverbs 13:15-25

Notes

Our Daily Walk

Trust and Obey

"Trust in the Lord with all thine heart; and lean not unto thine own understanding."

Proverbs 3:5

Every day for the first month of school, when telling a student my expectations his first response was, "Why?"

"Because I said so," I'm sure was my response at least once or twice.

After building a relationship with the student, I realized that he wasn't trying to be defiant or disrespectful to me. "Why?" had become a habit for him. He had developed a distrust of the adults in his life.

One day I vividly remember him standing by me. He asked me what he should do next. I gave him instructions, and his response again, "Why?"

I responded, "Do you trust me?"

"Yes," he said.

"Do you think I would have you do anything to hurt you or that would be unfair?" I asked.

"No," he replied.

"I care about you, so there is no need for you to ask me "Why?" every time I give you directions," I explained. That seemed to resonate with him because from that day on, he no longer asked me why. He had come to trust me.

Proverbs tells us to trust in God and not our own understanding. (Proverbs 3:5) Just like the boy, we feel the need to understand the outcome or the purpose of the challenges in our lives. Too often we want to reason and figure out why things are going the way they are before we move forward. Our life experiences may cause us to doubt God's presence and love for us. That is what Satan wants. Trusting in God shows that we believe He loves us and will fulfill His purpose without us having to know all the details before we move forward with obedience. Trust is key to any relationship, especially with Christ Jesus. We must not forget God is faithful!

"For therein is the righteousness of God revealed from faith to faith: as it is written: The just shall live by faith." Romans 1:17

Dear Lord Jesus,

Thank You for giving Your life for me. I know that You care for me, so I throw all my cares on You today. I trust You have a purpose for the challenges that I am facing right now. I choose to draw nearer to You and not allow the "Whys?" to prevent me from moving forward to fulfill Your will for my life. I rest in You completely and choose to trust You wholeheartedly. In Jesus name, Amen.

Reading Text – 1 Kings 18:1-16

NOTES

____

____

____

____

____

____

____

____

OUR DAILY WALK

HIGH EXPECTATIONS

"Because it is written, Be ye holy; for I am holy."

1 Peter 1:16

I had been on a medical leave. At the end of my first week back, one of my conscientious students confided in me, "Ever since you came back my stress levels have gone up. It's not as bad as my meltdown earlier in the year. You remember?"

"Oh my!" I responded as I drew closer to her. "I'm sorry that I have caused you more stress."

"I don't mean it bad. I know you are veteran teacher and have higher expectations than most. I want to be perfect, so it stresses me," explained the student.

I couldn't apologize because standards must be taught and mastered for student growth. "You know if you ask me for help, I will help you. Right?" I reminded her.

God's Word sets forth very specific guidelines for us to follow. For example, Noah was given a materials list and measurements from God for building the ark. Moses was given specific instructions on how to build the tabernacle, what materials were to be used, sacrificial qualifications, and details of the priests' clothing and duties. God is a god of details!

God has requirements for us that are referenced in the Old and New Testaments – fear the Lord, walk in all his ways, "love him, and serve the Lord thy God with all thy heart and with all thy soul…keep the commandments of the Lord." (Deuteronomy 10:12-13) Those are high expectation, especially since He requires our ALL. If we don't walk in the Spirit moment by moment, we may become overwhelmed and look at God's standards as too rigorous. God never commands us to do anything that is impossible. He is readily available to lift us up and give us what we need if we ask. High expectations are for our good and as they are met satisfy our Savior.

"For this is the love of God, that we keep his commandments: and his commandments are not grievous." 1 John 5:3

Dear Heavenly Father,

Thank You for the Word of God that gives me Your expectations. Forgive me for falling short. I know that Your commands are for my good. I love You with all my heart, soul, mind, and strength. I yield to You and seek Your empowerment to be holy as You are holy. I rest in faith believing that Your commands are not grievous. I submit afresh to You. In Jesus' name, Amen.

Reading Text- Genesis 6

NOTES

Our Daily Walk

Trouble with a Hug

"Come unto me, all ye that labour and are heavy laden, and I will give you rest."

Matthew 11:28

It had been a rough day! As I was dismissing students to buses, a stinker of a student, asked if he could hug me. He had been removed from class for misbehaving and disrupting others, so I was shocked when he asked. I said, "Of course." He smiled and gave me a quick hug on his way out to busses.

Soon after that exchange, the students and I discussed how we could greet differently each morning. I asked the students for their input. There were not many responses, but that same young man interjected, "I don't know about everyone else, but I'm going to hug you."

That sounds warm and fuzzy, but it is not easy to hug back when a student is unkind and disobedient. At that point, all I could think about was the love of my Savior. The Comforter hugs me and gives me peace every single day. I don't deserve it, but He loves me. Jesus has called us to come to Him with our struggles. We are not perfect and often like my student we repeat the same offenses or struggle with the same negative mindsets. Jesus calls us to come as we are, and He will give us rest. He does not deny us a hug. Paul reminded Titus, the young preacher, that we have all been "foolish, disobedient, deceived…hateful…But after that the kindness and love of God our Savior toward man appeared… according to his mercy he saved us…" (Titus 3:3-5)

Praise God for His mercy! I fear that like the mischievous student many want hugs from Jesus but continue to live displeasing to Him. Jesus showed compassion on the adulterous woman when the religious men wanted her stoned. As her accusers walked away in shame of their own sins, Jesus told her, "… go, and sin no more." (John 8:11) He showed mercy and love with no condemnation but expected her to stop her practice of sin. As we seek His forgiveness and choose a godly path for our life, His hugs are more intimate and comforting. Trouble or not, squeeze Him tightly and allow Him to wrap His arms around you, too.

"… love the Lord your God, and to walk in all his ways, and to keep his commandments, and to cleave unto him, and to serve him with all your heart and with all your soul." Joshua 22:5b

Dear Heavenly Father,

Thank You for forgiving me and providing me with Your comfort and grace. I choose to cling to You. Thank You for not denying me Your hugs. I love You. In Jesus' name. Amen.

Reading Text – Psalm 46

NOTES

Our Daily Walk

He's Still Working on Me

"For it is God which worketh in you both to will and to do of his good pleasure."

Philippians 2:13

As I contemplate this past school year, I'm glad it is over. I now purposefully look for new possibilities for next year and anticipate better things. I must admit it has been a rocky year. I know that like other years each blunder and success has molded me into a better person, and by God's grace an improved teacher. Thank God, He is still working on me.

He is the potter! I am the clay! As I think of the Master kneading the clay with strong but loving hands, it makes me cringe. About the time I think things are where they should be with my walk in Christ and teaching, I find out differently. I have not yet attained! I think I just fell off the Potter's wheel. He had to place me back up on the wheel to mold and recreate and then to spin me around and around to refine me. Dizzy, disoriented, but I'm securely held by the Potter with the hope and trust that He will make me what He wants me to be, Christlike.

Most of us think we are pretty good at what we do. We think we are at least as good a teacher and Christian as those we are around. What really matters is what does Christ see? We are warned by Paul not to deceive ourselves or to think we are above failing or falling in our Christian walk. (1 Corinthians 3:18) We must see ourselves as God sees us!

I know I fall way short when I rely solely on my own abilities and self-will! (That's when I've fallen off the Potter's wheel.) I'm grateful that when I confess my faults and humble myself to be made into the person that He wants me to be that He forgives me. (That's when I'm placed back on the Potter's wheel.) The victory comes through Christ Jesus because of what He provides for me. He knows exactly what needs changed and reformed in my teaching and personal life. I yield my life to be molded and made into the person and vessel that He is pleased to use. I find peace and contentment in knowing He is still working on me!

"And the vessel that he made of clay was marred in the hand of the potter: so he made it again another vessel, as seemed good to the potter to make it." Jeremiah 18:4

Dear Heavenly Father,

Thank You for the lessons learned this school year. I thank You that you are still working on me to make me what YOU want me to be. As I look forward to next school year, help me to draw from the lessons learned, and by my mistakes and successes. Above all else help me to be well-pleasing in Your sight for Your honor and glory. In Jesus' name I pray, Amen.

Reading Text – Romans 9:14-26

NOTES

Our Daily Walk

Sanitize and Sanctify

"That he might sanctify and cleanse it with the washing of water by the word,"

Ephesians 5:26

Clean! Clean! Clean! While many schools remained in virtual mode, our corporation chose to have in-person classes. Our major focus in our first meeting was discussing how essential it was for us to follow protocol: Sanitize desktops every time there was a switch of students and before dismissal. On any classroom transition, students should use hand sanitizer before entering the next area or classroom. Before lunch, students should wash their hands with soap and water. After recess, wash with soap and water or use sanitizer before entering the classroom. Due diligence was essential to lessen the chance of spreading the virus and other germs.

Hand sanitizer and desktop sanitizer with towelettes were provided for each classroom. Extra time was given between transitions for following the cleaning expectations. As the year went on, less and less were following the protocols. After all, it took more time and was a pain. On more than one occasion, students commented that they hadn't been expected to clean their hands as often. My response, "That's fine but to remain healthy and in the classroom, we will use sanitizer each time we leave my area." We had a routine, and once I forgot to pull out the sanitizer students reminded me.

I was grateful for their reminder and want to remind you to be diligent about your walk with Christ Jesus. Just like our corporation provides the cleaning supplies, God offers all that we need for our purification in His Word. The psalmist in Psalm 119:11 proclaimed, "Thy word have I hid in mine heart, that I might not sin against thee." It is the Word of God that cleanses us and keeps us from sin. We must not become too busy to study the Word, or we become more susceptible to bad attitudes, old habits, and yield to temptations. Don't become complacent and disengaged with the process that leads to victory and safety in Christ Jesus. Don't grow weary in reading the Word of God, praying, and building your faith. Daily sanctify and prepare to enter His presence in holiness and purity.

"...be diligent that ye may be found of him in peace, without spot, and blameless." 2 Peter 3:14b

Dear Lord Jesus,

Thank You for providing all that I need to remain clean by Your Word. Forgive me where I have skipped time with You. Help me not to be deceived in believing I'm exempt from old habits and sins. I choose to be diligent about seeking You and Your righteousness for Your name's sake. Amen.

Reading Text – Psalm 51

Notes

____

____

____

____

____

____

____

____

____

Our Daily Walk

Pay Attention

"He that hath ears to hear, let him hear."

Matthew 11:15

"Okay, boys and girls have a seat, and we'll get started," I instructed. No one seemed to listen.

Quietly I said, "If you can hear me, clap once," a few students clapped once. I repeated it three more times before 100% of the students clapped and became silent. The excitement of the day made it difficult for students to give me their attention. I had to use that technique quite a few times that day.

Sometimes we are more focused on school duties, activities, family, or personal struggles and find it difficult to hear the voice of God. Other times, we listen to the voice of others and become clouded about God's will. In Numbers 22, God originally told Balaam not to go with the princes of Moab but then told him to go ahead and follow them. God knew Balaam wanted to go with the men but told him to be sure to listen to Him.

God was not happy with Balaam's choice to follow the Moabites. He sent an angel to delay Balaam's meeting with Balak. Balaam's donkey could see the angel, but he could not. The donkey tried to avoid the angel three times. First, the donkey went off the path. Next, the it crushed Balaam's foot against a wall. Lastly, the donkey dropped to the ground and refused to move. Each time Balaam hit the donkey with his staff. The third time, the donkey literally spoke to Balaam. Then Balaam's eyes were opened to see the angel of the Lord with a sword in his hand. It took the donkey speaking and the angel revealing himself to Balaam to finally get his attention.

God placed the angel as an obstacle in Balaam's path. When there are obstacles in our way, we must take time to seek and listen for God's voice. We must not allow the circumstances or chatter of others to distract or lead us astray. It's highly unlikely that God will ever use a talking donkey or an armored angel to get our attention. Regardless, be alert! Pay attention and listen the voice of the Lord.

"So that thou incline thine ear unto wisdom, and apply thine heart to understanding;" Proverbs 2:2

Dear Heavenly Father,

Thank You for continuing to speak to me through Your Word by the Holy Spirit.

Forgive me when I have been too stubborn to listen to You. Help me to pay attention more carefully when life gets chaotic and trials come my way. I choose to get quiet and listen to Your still small voice. Thank You for Your patience with me. I love You. In Jesus' name, Amen.

Reading Text – Numbers 22:18-41

NOTES

Our Daily Walk

Success God's Way

"This book of the law shall not depart out of thy mouth; but thou shalt meditate therein day and night, that thou mayest observe to do according to all that is written therein: for then thou shalt make thy way prosperous, and then thou shalt have good success."

Joshua 1:8

"Is it a full moon?" I asked.

"No, I don't think so," responded a colleague.

"It's been a rough couple of days. I sure hope things are better tomorrow," I said.

Then it dawned on me, the last few days I hadn't spent much time with Jesus. My devotional times had been extremely short, only about five minutes each with eyebrow prayers. My mind had been cluttered with what I had to do before students arrived, my meetings, and the calls that I needed to make to parents. By neglecting my spiritual food, I was on the struggle bus and things were amiss in my classroom. I was tired and frustrated because I was relying solely on my own experiences without the power of the Holy Spirit.

I was reminded of King Saul. When Samuel, the prophet, was late for the customary sacrifice, King Saul decided he would perform the sacrifice. After all, he had watched Samuel and had the skills to do the task. Everything looked the same but without God's hand and approval. King Saul lost his kingship because he disobeyed and then acted on his own when he sacrificed without regards to God's plan. Far worse than losing a kingship, he was left without the presence of the Spirit of the Lord. (1 Samuel 16:14)

Kids will be kids, and there will be good days and bad days. The more time I spend in the Word of God the better days I have. Notice that I said, "I have." It may not change the behavior of the students but being filled with the Spirit who gives peace, guidance, and strength on those hard days makes all the difference in the world. His Word prevents me from doing or saying things that I regret and provides the light for me to follow when interacting with students and staff.

"Thy word is a lamp unto my feet, and a light unto my path." Psalm 119:105

Dear Heavenly Father,

Forgive me for not spending more time in the Bible. I choose to meditate upon what You have provided in Your Word. Help me not be consumed by the activities of life without considering Your plan and will for me. I'm thankful for the ministry of children, so I call upon You to help me meet the challenges of teaching. I choose to walk in the Spirit of God this day. In Jesus' name, Amen.

Reading Text – 1 Samuel 15:10-26

NOTES

____

____

____

____

____

____

____

____

Our Daily Walk

Put a String on Your Finger

"I will remember the works of the Lord: surely I will remember thy wonders of old."

Psalm 77:11

"Don't forget to fill out your agenda," I reminded the students.

"I forgot to study last night, Mrs. Pearcy," a couple of students admitted frantically the next day. Students' agendas are used to remind them of assignments but too often they refuse to use them or just forget.

The children of Israel didn't have agendas but were told to remember God's goodness and commandments by binding them upon their hands, placing them on their foreheads, and writing them upon their doorposts. In Numbers 15, God told Moses to have the children of Israel sew a blue ribbon in the fringes of their garments as a reminder throughout their generations. He said that it would be a reminder for them to obey the commandments and follow holiness instead of after their own heart and eyes. It was to remind them to be holy unto God. As I researched the use of the word "remember" I found that most passages had the following themes: Remember the Lord! Remember the works of the Lord! Remember His commandments! Remember His judgments!

We may use an agenda, a string around the finger, post-it notes, and electronic gadgets to remind us of things in our day-to-day life. Whatever it takes we need to remember Christ and His holiness in all that we do. There are a few things we can do to help us to remember our Almighty God: First, set aside a specific time each day to read the Word of God. Reading the Bible is the key to prompt our memory and renew our minds in Christ Jesus. Next, regularly attend church. A pastor is God's minister who uses the Word to remind us of God's gift, His works, the commandments, and even His judgments. The scriptures say, "…faith cometh by hearing and hearing by the Word of God." (Romans 10:17) We must hear it to create a memory. Finally, we can be like the psalmist David and hide it in our heart so that we don't sin against God. (Psalm 119:11) All these things are ways to help us remember, and they are pleasing to the Father. String on the finger or not, let us not forget about Jesus, His works, His expectations, and finally His judgments!

Remember his marvellous works that he hath done; his wonders, and the judgments of his mouth;" Psalm 105:5

Dear Heavenly Father,

Help me to remember the important things of life, according to Your Word. I choose to view things from Your point of view. I thank You for reminding me of Your goodness and grace. Help me to retain Your Word when I read, attend church, and memorize verses. I choose to remember You for the God that You are! Thank You for Your wonderful works. In Jesus' name, Amen.

Reading Text – Numbers 15:37-41

NOTES

____

____

____

____

____

____

Section 8 – Keep It Positive

Keep It Positive
Praises

"I will call upon the Lord, who
is worthy to be praised: ..."

Psalm 18:3a

The Heavenly Father is worthy of all my praise.
He saved me and keeps me along life's way.
Jesus died on the cross as the ransom for all.
I'm glad He waited for me to heed His sweet call.
The gift of His Son Jesus is more than I deserve.
I must praise and worship daily with no reserve!

Praise and glory to the Father for all He has done.
Forgiveness He has granted for a life undone.
Deliverance from a life full of bondage and sin,
Healing for a soul broken from sickness within,
Christ Jesus died to accomplish all without denial.
Honor and praise for His grace will never be final!

I praise Him for salvation, deliverance, and health.
I have no doubt of His love and unspeakable wealth.
Christ Jesus is willing and able to meet ev'ry need.
With humble heart, I approach Him on bended knee.
I've found that He answers and gives many desires.
His merciful, gracious, compassionate heart I admire.

Joy unspeakable and honor to my Great Savior.
Grateful for His goodness and unearned favor,
Promises of assurance that He'll never leave me,
Comfort, joy, and peace within me flow freely.
Confidence acquired from His promises fulfilled.
Faith built as I trust Him, a heart that is thrilled.

Praise, honor, and glory to the Great Holy One!
Tributes of worship to Him and His begotten Son
Regardless, of life's trials I will lift up my voice.
To acclaim Him and extol Him is my first choice.
Glorifying and exalting Christ to the uttermost.
Adoration to the Father, Son, and Holy Ghost!

"Whom having not seen, ye love; in whom, though now ye see him not, yet believing, ye rejoice with joy unspeakable and full of glory:" 1 Peter 1:8

Dear Heavenly Father,

Words cannot describe the praise You deserve! My joy is full thinking of the salvation and grace You have bestowed on me. Be honored and glorified this day in all that I do. In Jesus' name, Amen.

Bible Reading – Psalm 145

NOTES

Keep It Positive

I'm His Favorite

"The Lord thy God in the midst of thee is mighty;...he will rejoice over thee with joy; he will rest in his love, he will joy over thee with singing."

Zephaniah 3:17

"I'm her favorite," proclaimed one student to his classmates. I just listened as this troubled little boy shared his feelings.

Another student close by me, in his shy, quiet way glanced at me and turned slightly. "Then, I'm her second."

I assured him that he is my favorite too.

I thought of the story of the Prodigal Son. It was the troubled son that was celebrated. He had taken his inheritance and spent it all riotously. He became so destitute that he returned to his father's house to be a servant, but instead his father threw him a party. He was given a ring on his finger, a robe on his back, and shoes on his feet. The faithful son returned home and wondered what was going on. Jealousy arose when he was told that his prodigal brother was being celebrated. He had been faithful to work for his father and felt it unfair. The loving father expressed his appreciation to the faithful son but couldn't help but rejoice at his prodigal son's return. The father's love was the same for both sons, yet the fairness of the father was questioned.

Just like the trustworthy son, responsible students may not understand our judgments when dealing with a troubled classmate. They may question our fairness, but they should never doubt our love. Spiritually, whether we have been the prodigal or the faithful child of God, we must understand that His love is never changing. God favors those who obey and walk in His ways. At the same time, He loves sinners, and His angels rejoice over those who repent of their sins. Whether the faithful one or a repentant sinner, His delight comes when individuals are drawing nearer to the Father. Those who please Him are His favorites! As I surrender to please Him, I can say, "I'm His favorite." Because He loves me.

"For whoso findeth me findeth life, and shall obtain favour of the Lord." Proverbs 8:35

Dear Heavenly Father,

Thank You for Your unchanging love! Forgive me where I have questioned Your judgment toward me and others. I know that You love all of us equally, and You will bless those that seek Your face. I choose to love my students in such a way that they trust my judgment. Help me to recognize those that are faithful to do their work and praise them while celebrating those that need encouraged to do right. I love You and choose Your ways above my ways. In Jesus' name, Amen.

Bible Reading – 1 John 4

NOTES

____

____

____

____

____

____

KEEP IT POSITIVE

THE CAN'T FAMILY FUNERAL

"Not that we are sufficient of ourselves to think any thing as of ourselves; but our sufficiency is of God;"

2 Corinthians 3:5

Great stress comes at the beginning of a new school year, and I find myself feeling like I can't keep up. Satan would have me to believe that I can't do it. I know better than that and have drawn great strength from the promises of the Word of God. As Paul said, "...and when I am weak, then am I strong." (2 Corinthians 12:10) I'm a veteran and know that I can teach effectively, but that does not keep the "Can'ts" from trying to sneak into my life.

I was reminded this week of a funeral that I held a few years back in one of my classes. Students too often would say, "I can't." They had failed repeatedly in prior grades. Some would cry to me, "I can't! I've never been able to do it before. I can't do it, Mrs. Pearcy."

I would reassure the students that I would never ask them to do something that they couldn't do. I felt that I had to do something to improve their attitudes and thoughts about school. I had my students write down all the things that they thought they could not do. Each one of us placed an index card full of "I Can'ts" in a shoebox (casket). After briefly discussing the purpose behind writing the cards, I told the students that we were having a Can't family funeral. With a shovel in hand, I led the class outside of our portable and dug a hole. I placed the shoebox in the hole and covered it with dirt. Two sticks were found, and a cross was made to mark the spot. I held a brief funeral service and had the students repeat a promise in unison.

I propose that we bury our Can'ts and say, "I solemnly promise to never use "Can't" as an excuse because I can do all things through Christ. (Philippians 4:13) I promise to listen to new and old ideas to improve my teaching and refuse to believe I "Can't" use them. When I feel like I "Can't" I will wait on the Lord to renew my strength (Isaiah 40:31) and not hesitate to ask a colleague for help. I solemnly vow not to be snared by saying, "I Can't." I trust God for peace and the ability to do anything that I set my mind to do. The Can'ts are buried and can no longer control me."

"I can do all things through Christ which strengtheneth me." Philippians 4:13

Dear Heavenly Father,

I bury all the Can'ts in my life today. I rely on You to meet the demands on my job, family, and church. I claim Your victory through the Word of God today and refuse to allow the Can'ts to control my life anymore. Thank You, Lord Jesus, Amen

(*The Can't Funeral was not my original idea. I don't recall where I read it, but I developed the idea.)

Bible Reading –Proverbs 6

NOTES

Keep It Positive

Keeping Rhythm

"Praise him upon the loud cymbals: praise him upon the high sounding cymbals. Let every thing that hath breath praise the LORD. Praise ye the LORD."

Psalm 150:5-6

It was refreshing to watch a student walking down the hallway rhythmically snapping his fingers and walking with an upbeat to his steps. When he drew closer to me, I asked if he had a song in his heart. "Yep," as he kept his beat and continued to his classroom.

I don't know that student's story, but he was unlike most students that are walking alone in the hallway. Most walk with their heads down and seem to be troubled or pre-occupied in deep thought. Doesn't that sound just like us?

Lately, my thoughts had been on the struggles of those around me, including myself. I recognized that unconsciously I had stopped listening to my Christian music while traveling to and from school. I had been contemplating the trials of my personal life, struggles with students in the classroom, learning plans for the day, and often praying for so many with needs. It is okay to do that, but I realized that that practice had drained my heart of its song. I needed some spiritual fuel beyond my Bible reading. I needed some rhythm and a song.

There are over 150 references to singing in the Bible. There are over 60 in the Book of Psalm alone. The lives of the psalmist were not without trials, but they learned to write down their praise and sing with musical instruments keeping the beat as they sang. Music is good for the soul, especially when the lyrics are filled with God's Word and truth. The Spirit has used the words and rhythm of songs to prepare my heart to receive what He has prepared for me. Often, I sing along. Other times I keep beat to the music. Sometimes as I listen intently, I cry to think of God's grace and His ultimate sacrifice for me. More times than not, when it's time to walk into school my joy is full, and I can say, "I have a song in my heart." I don't have much rhythm in my step these days, but praising the Lord sure puts an unspeakable joy and a pitter patter back in my heart.

"And he hath put a new song in my mouth, even praise unto our God:..." Psalm 40:3a

Dear Heavenly Father,

Thank You for the Spirit of God who brings joy to my heart. I praise You for the songwriters that have used the truth of Your Word to create music that touches my heart. Help me to be more like the student who had a song in his heart rather than like the Israelites who put their harps on the willow trees in defeat. I choose to have a new song in my mouth daily. In Jesus's name. Amen.

Bible Reading – Psalm 149

NOTES

____

____

____

____

____

____

____

____

Keep It Positive

GLADTOWN

"Rejoice in the Lord alway: and I again I say, Rejoice."

Philippians 4:4

In class one day, we watched a "CNN Student News" clip that addressed loneliness. The doctor who was interviewed has done a study with brain research that shows that a simple HELLO can make a difference to those spoken to. He stated that making eye to eye contact and saying "Hello" can bring a change to a lonely heart. I suspect he would say the same about a simple smile.

While considering the thought of happiness, Pollyanna (a movie character) came to mind. "Pollyanna" is a 1960 Walt Disney Movie.[6] It has a good message. It is about an orphan who was sent to live with her aunt. She found a lot of grumpy, unhappy people in her

[6] Walt Disney, *Pollyanna* (Burbank, CA: Buena Vista Home Video Dept, CS, 1997), VHS

new town: The preacher of the town was rough on the people every Sunday, Pollyanna's aunt was difficult, an older woman always complained of sickness, and an old grumpy man always chased the kids off his property. Everyone seemed to complain. Pollyanna came to town and changed all of that, a little at a time. She was happy and friendly to all. She was able to change a very unhappy community into GLADTOWN. It's a fictional story, but there were some truths shared. One is that there are several passages in the Bible that have the word "glad" in them.

I did a word search of my own - happy, rejoice, cheer, glad, and joy - and found that there are over 600 passages with those words in the Bible. I found it interesting that not many passages were without reference to difficulties or life trials. This happiness or cheerfulness is not based on the circumstances of our life but the understanding of God's goodness and presence in our life. If I truly rejoice in who God is to me and what he has given to me, I can be genuinely happy!

Be happy! Lift people up and don't bring them down! Think about your conversations and your disposition. Yes, we will have days that we struggle, but on most days where do you find yourself? Count your blessings and rejoice, for our God is good! Create a GLADTOWN and enjoy those whom the Lord has placed in your life.

"I will praise thee, O LORD, with my whole heart; I will shew forth all thy marvelous works. I will be glad and rejoice in thee: I will sing praise to thy name, O thou most High." Psalm 9:1-2

Dear Heavenly Father,

Thank You for giving me a wonderful support system. They bring me joy! I praise You for Your goodness and grace. When difficulty comes my way, I choose to focus on Your promises fulfilled and those yet to come. Help me to exemplify a genuine attitude of joy and gladness so that I may be an encouragement to others for Your name's sake. In Jesus' name, Amen.

Bible Reading – Proverbs 3

Notes

KEEP IT POSITIVE

GLORIOUS FACE

"... looking stedfastly on him, saw his face as it had been the face of an angel."

Acts 6:15

"You look happy today!" Observed a colleague.

"Are you okay? You don't seem yourself today," asked a concerned teammate.

"I like coming to your class. You're always happy to see me," a student said as she entered the classroom.

Similar words have been spoken to me, and I have said them to others. As we read the expressions on faces daily, our face is being observed too. Are we glowing or displaying gloom? Do our faces show that we are walking closely with Jesus, or have we allowed circumstances and challenges to consume our thoughts which in turn may show on our faces?

The thought of me having a glorious face first came to my attention when I read about the martyrdom of Stephen in Acts 6-7. He was proclaiming the Gospel and being falsely accused. The scripture says, "the council...saw his face as it had been the face of an angel." I'm not quite sure what the face of an angel would look like, but I suspect there was a glow to it. If it wasn't a glow, it must have been a peaceful and loving look of kindness towards those who were persecuting him. As Stephen was dying, he asked that those men be forgiven. Only a man walking in the presence and light of the Lord could have the face of an angel like that.

Moses had been with God on Mt. Sinai to get the second set of commandments. When he returned to the Israelites, his face was aglow. He had been with Jehovah God! It tells us in the New Testament that during the transfiguration that Jesus' face shined like the sun and his garments were as white as light. Jesus was in the presence of His Heavenly Father, and the disciples were witnesses. Just like Jesus, Moses, and Stephen, it is the presence of God that will permeate on our faces with His glory as we wisely walk in His ways. His glory will become our glory as we live in His presence.

"Thou wilt shew me the path of life; in thy presence is fulness of joy;..." Psalm 16:11a

Dear Lord Jesus,

Forgive me for not always walking in Your presence. I choose to draw closer to You and to draw my wisdom from Your Word. I know that students and adults are watching me. Help me to display happiness and contentment rather than frustration and pain. I choose to live above the circumstances and challenges that would steal my joy. I choose to have a genuine smile of contentment and peace because You are the God of all hope and peace. I lean on You and trust You to shine through me today for Your honor and glory in Christ Jesus. Amen

Bible Reading – Exodus 34:28-35

NOTES

KEEP IT POSITIVE

CELEBRATE

"I will bless the LORD at all times: his praise shall continually be in my mouth."

Psalm 34:1

It is key for us to celebrate even the seemingly small successes of our students and teaching. We can get bogged down with the busyness of teaching and focus on the extensive needs of students and grow discouraged quite easily unless we purpose to praise the Lord. One teacher celebrated by sharing the following:

Celebration One: "One of my students has been chronically behind on assignments. Day after day, I have tried to work with her to get her to start completing her work at home, even one task would be improvement. Admittedly, her home life is a shambles. Her weekly reading log has been an area where she had accumulated zero after zero. Imagine the joy and celebration when this week, she had actually completed her reading! She didn't fully finish the task because she hasn't competed the log, BUT at least she read. That may sound small, but it was a huge step and we celebrated. Maybe next week, she'll feel encouraged to have the reading and the log finished."

Celebration Two: "Another student who was out of control is now on medication. It's a HUGE difference. We've gone from missing work and out of control behavior to focus and bodily control. I believe he's so much happier because he is able to focus and participate. I am so thankful for the good conversations with mom and for the wonderful change for him. It's a solid win for everyone."

In Psalm 126, there was praise when the Israelites came out of captivity. They rejoiced, sang, and praised the Lord. Because the Israelites celebrated, the onlookers recognized that the Lord had done great things for them. The psalmist wrote in verse three, "The Lord hath done great things for us; whereof we are glad." (verse 3) As a believer, we must take a biblical approach and realize that our praise influences those around us.

Often teachers are hesitant to share successes because others may perceive them as bragging. It is not bragging. It is essential to celebrate student victories. When we see our students succeed, there is joy! Whether great or small, we are to give thanks in all things. Small victories lead to greater victories so celebrate them all. What wonderful thing is the Lord doing in your classroom? Speak up! You may influence those who are struggling to celebrate rather than complain.

"In every thing give thanks: for this is the will of God in Christ Jesus concerning you." 1 Thessalonians 5:18

Dear Heavenly Father,

Thank You for giving me joy! You are Lord above all, and I choose to exalt You. Help me to speak up in the staff meeting when there is time for celebrations. May others know that I'm grateful for all things that can glorify Your name. In Jesus' name, Amen.

Bible Reading – Psalm 34

NOTES

____

____

____

____

____

____

____

SECTION 9 – **PERSEVERE**

PERSEVERE
JOYFULLY FLEXIBLE

"...for I have learned, in whatsoever state I am, therewith to be content."

Philippians 4:11

"I'm so excited. I got my plans done for the next two weeks," said my zealous colleague.

"Did you see the e-mail this morning? Next week, school pictures are sometime on Tuesday. We must have the monthly fire drill before Friday, and we need to make sure to complete the technology safety lessons. Don't forget that sometime next week they will need to pull some of our students for testing," I said to inform her.

"Are you kidding?" responded the colleague with frustration.

"When you become a teacher, your middle name becomes Flexible," I replied.

Inclement weather, convocations, extra rehearsals, corporation programs, and other circumstances can require that we adapt our plans. Sometimes we have a few days to make those adjustments, but other times it may be minutes before school starts. It's how we handle the situation that will make the difference in our week or day. It can be stressful to say the least if we allow it.

Our daily approach to life and our mindset will determine how we handle the things that are out of our control. The Apostle Paul had learned to be content in any situation. He had been poor and rich. He had been free and imprisoned. (Philippians 4:11-12) His most victorious writings were written while he was in jail. His imprisonment was more serious than anything that we face, yet Paul could be content because he put his eyes on things above and not the everyday things. He set out to seek the Lord and please Him in everything that he did. In Colossians 3, Paul gives us instructions on how to obey those in charge of us and then follows with "do it heartedly, as to the Lord." (vs.23) If we have set our focus on pleasing the Lord, then we will be more flexible when a wrench gets thrown into our agenda. Flexibility with a godly attitude of contentment is far better than being stressed and grumbling about the things we cannot change.

"And whatsoever ye do, do it heartily, as to the Lord, and not unto men:" Colossians 3:23

Dear Lord Jesus,

Thank You for giving me the best job in the world. I choose to teach wholeheartedly to please you. Help me guard my attitude when my plans get changed by others. I choose to find my contentment in You no matter what comes my way. Help me to be joyfully flexible rather than stubbornly resentful. I love You and choose more than anything to please You. Give me strength this day. In your name, Amen.

Bible Reading – Colossians 1

NOTES

____

____

____

____

____

____

____

PERSEVERE

LIMITATIONS? LET GOD

"Now therefore go, and I will be with thy mouth, and teach thee what thou shalt say."

Exodus 4:12

In my second year of teaching, I watched a shy student blossom into quite the leader. His mom shared that with four years of speech therapy, her son struggled with his self-confidence. His first boost of confidence came when he won the election for Student Council. Later in the year, I had to escort a student to the office for a recess incident. When I got back to my room, that young man was sitting in my chair at the front of the room reading the novel that I had started earlier in the week. All eyes were on him and not a peep could be heard. I was amazed. I said, "I'm so proud of you all. Did Mr. Woods tell you to read to the class, Brian?"

"Oh, no. I told everyone to have a seat, and I'd read to them like you do every day," he said, "and they all listened as I read." I would have never guessed that young man would become such a leader.

As I read about Moses, I thought of my former student. Moses was called of God to lead the Israelites out of Egypt, but he lacked confidence. God demonstrated how He would perform wondrous works to convince Pharaoh through Moses. He would transform his rod into a snake, turn his hand leprous and clean again, and change water into blood. Even after seeing those miracles, Moses told God he couldn't speak well enough to approach Pharaoh. God wasn't pleased but provided a mouthpiece for Moses, his brother, Aaron. From the beginning of Exodus to the end, God was faithful, and Moses grew to be a great leader because he followed the call of God.

Teaching is God's calling and doesn't go without challenges. Whether we are asked to be a teacher leader, teach the most misbehaved class in the school, create lessons for a significantly diverse group of learners, or work closely with obstinate parents, God will provide like He did for Moses. Since He has called us, He will prevail over our limitations. Even if God chooses to put others beside us to assist us and uses our few strengths to complete His work in and through us. Limitations? Let God prevail!

*"Faithful is he that calleth you, who also will do it."
1 Thessalonians 5:24*

Dear Heavenly Father,

Thank You for calling me to teach. Forgive me when I use my insecurities as an excuse when it gets difficult. I choose to rely fully on You because you are faithful. In Jesus' name, Amen.

Bible Reading – Exodus 4

NOTES

____

____

____

____

____

____

____

____

Persevere

Coping with Failure

"There is therefore now no condemnation to them which are in Christ Jesus, who walk not after the flesh, but after the Spirit."

Romans 8:1

After failing atrociously, I struggled for several days to overcome depression and my failure. Notice, I said "my" failure. At the beginning, I went through the process of blaming it on others and the circumstances. I could justify my reasoning, too. However, for me to overcome the depression and disappointment, I had to come face to face with the fact that I failed to meet expectations and, in the process, failed others. Taking ownership of my own shortcomings was very humbling.

As I shared my feelings of disappointment, my good friends consoled me and refused to allow me to claim my failure. I never expected anything less of them. They reminded me of all my hard work and extra efforts. They came up with all the excuses that I had already dealt with in the privacy of my home. Highlighting the wonderful things people had to say about me should have been validation enough, but it was not. No, I had to face the awful truth. Numbers don't lie. Failure for sure!

Struggling with condemnation, I confessed my failure to the One who matters most, Christ Jesus. My failure was not sin, but I had allowed it to control my life, and that was sin. I asked others to forgive me and forgave myself. I knew it was time to move on and no longer allowed that failure to control me.

In the Bible, Joshua and David went to prayer about their failures. When the men of Israel lost the battle at Ai, Joshua prayed and asked God how he could allow such a thing to happen. God told him to get off his face and deal with the problem. David prayed and fasted seven days and nights as his illegitimate son was dying. As soon as his baby died, he got up, washed, and ate. He confessed his sin but could do nothing about God's judgment in taking his baby boy. He knew it was time to move on.

By these two examples, I have been encouraged to pray, deal with the problem, and move on to the next challenge. Failures will occur. By God's grace, they will help me draw closer to Him and become a better teacher for His sake.

"If we confess our sins, he is faithful and just to forgive us our sins, and to cleanse us from all unrighteousness." 1 John 1:9

Dear Heavenly Father,

Please forgive me for my pride. My successes are only by Your grace, and my failures are a reminder that You are still working on me. For that I am grateful! I know that teaching is Your call in my life, and I choose to do it effectively. When I fail, I choose to pray, learn from my failure, and move on in my teaching. I know that when I am weak then you are strong. Be exalted! In Jesus' name, Amen.

Bible Reading – Joshua 7

NOTES

____

____

____

____

____

____

Persevere

Potential for Good

"And we know that all things work together for good to them that love God, and to them who are the called according to his purpose."

Romans 8:28

It was the end of my first year of teaching. All alone, I sat with tears as I initialed my student records and reflected on my school year. On the last day of school, two students had been suspended for fighting which was indicative of that year's challenges for me. The week before I received the status of my evaluation and was placed on an improvement plan. To say I was disappointed in myself would be an understatement.

Lysa Terkeurst wrote, "Disappointment holds the potential for so much good. But we'll only see it as good if we trust the heart of the Giver."[7] Disappointment may

---

[7] Lysa TerKeurst, *It's Not Supposed to be This Way*, Nashville: HarperCollins Christian Publishing, Inc, 2018. p.5.

be a gift from God that doesn't feel like a gift. I know in that moment in time, my disappointment did not feel like a gift, and I certainly could not see what good could come from it. It was God's way of conforming me into His image, and my failures caused me to seek Christ more fervently. As I reflect now, the Giver had a plan and knew my potential for good.

Throughout the Bible, men and women dealt with disappointments. Peter is a prime example of someone who failed and grieved over his denial of Jesus. He wept bitterly. He had humiliated himself that day. His disappointment was a gift that day because God had bigger plans for him. His brokenness eventually was used for good. Peter preached, proclaimed, and proved his faith in Christ Jesus on the day of Pentecost and for many years after. God knew Peter's potential for good.

Without a doubt, God knows our potential, too. Our disappointments are continual gifts from God that have a way of drawing us closer to Him. Humbling ourselves and yielding to Him daily is key. To the praise and glory of God, over the years I been honored by colleagues with teaching awards. In and through my disappointments, He saw my potential and has blessed beyond my imagination.

"Humble yourselves therefore under the mighty hand of God, that he may exalt you in due time:" 1 Peter 5:6

Dear Heavenly Father,

Thank You for continually working on me. I'm thankful that You are not done with me yet. I know that my failures allow You to conform and shape me into the teacher and person that You want me to be. They hurt so much and yet pressure me to meet Your expected potential for good. To You always and forever be all honor and praise! In Jesus' name, Amen.

Bible Reading – Luke 22:50 - 62

NOTES

____

____

____

____

____

____

____

____

Persevere

How Do You Eat an Elephant?

"Take therefore no thought for the morrow: for the morrow shall take thought for the things of itself. Sufficient unto the day is the evil thereof."

Matthew 6:34

When school year started, I attended a workshop and the presenter had so many great ideas. As the workshop continued over a couple of days, the information became overwhelming because there was so much to digest. The presenter became aware of the anxiety of many attending educators and made a very profound statement: "How do you eat an elephant? One bite at a time!" At times I feel like I have the entire elephant in my mouth! The past few months I have had to remind myself to "eat one bite at a time."

Ever get overwhelmed with all that is expected of you? Maybe it is the demands of teaching. Maybe it's keeping up with your family's needs. Maybe it is your ministry for Christ. For many of us, it is balancing all those things. Some might say you have too many pots in the fire! However, if it is what Christ has called you to do then you must live your life for Him and in His strength. Living moment by moment and relying heavily on the precepts of God will alleviate much of the stresses in this life.

As we try to balance all that Christ has called us to do, we must draw from His Word. Good sound advice is to live moment by moment, step by step, and yield each task of life to Christ. As I researched the Word of God, I found it interesting that none of the scriptures literally state to live moment by moment. However, they do tell us to take no thought for tomorrow (Matthew 6:34) and to walk wisely in our understanding of the will of the Lord. There is always an order to how things should be done. The Bible tells us that "the steps of a good man are ordered by the Lord" (Psalm 37:23) and that the Lord will direct his steps. It only makes sense that we should live life step by step and moment by moment. So, when that elephant gets stuck in your mouth and becomes too hard to swallow, stop, consider, and pull it out of your mouth. Eat it "one bite at a time!"

"A man's heart deviseth his way: but the LORD directeth his steps." Proverbs 16:9

Dear Heavenly Father,

Thank You for being my peace and strength in this overwhelming time. Forgive me for fretting about tomorrow. Help me to be satisfied in checking off one thing at a time on my lists. I commit my ways to You and ask You to help me take one bite at a time. I choose to please You in my teaching and all ministries that You have called me to do. I love You. In Jesus' name, Amen.

Bible Reading – Luke 12:22 – 34

NOTES

____

____

____

____

____

____

____

____

PERSEVERE

RESIGN OR RE-SIGN

"... be ye stedfast, unmoveable, always abounding in the work of the Lord, forasmuch as ye know that your labour is not in vain in the Lord."

1 Corinthians 15:58

I quit! I have had enough! Every new class brings its own challenges. Some years are more difficult than others. Last year may have been the most trying of all so I contemplated resignation more than once. Of course, that thought did not linger long when I was reminded of God's calling in my life. Passages of scripture guided me to reason, *"If I obey Christ's calling in my life, then I'll be pleasing the Father. I want to please my Savior more than anything else in this world! I am confident that if I remain faithful to His calling then He will finish the work in and through me."*

As a pastor's wife, of a small church, I find myself doing a lot of things. Often it is just because there are not enough people to step up currently. Understanding that reality does not keep me from growing discouraged and allowing thoughts of resignation. When those negative thoughts come, I consider the consequences of my resignation. First, if I quit serving and ministering then I will not fulfill God's will in my life, and He will be displeased. Second, if I quit and show a loss of faith in God and His promises, how will it affect my family and friends? If I say and I don't do, then I am a hypocrite like many other professing Christians. Those are reasons enough for me not to resign.

Almost as quickly as I think of resigning, I re-sign with determination to remain faithful to my Lord and Savior, Jesus Christ. I purpose with my heart to do all for His honor and glory. I claim the strength of the Lord and believe that He who started the work in me will complete it as I remain steadfast and unmovable. It's not about what others are or are not doing. It's about how I am responding to Christ's calling and my relationship with Him.

Just like one small mark defines the difference between resign and re-sign, one tiny thought entertained can be detrimental to our relationship with Christ. We can quit and forget God's calling and goodness, or we can re-sign and win the battle for His sake. We cannot allow the thoughts of resignation to nest in our thoughts. When life gets challenging, we may have to re-sign and re-sign and re-sign until we overcome the tiniest inkling of resignation.

"…he which hath begun a good work in you will perform it until the day of Jesus Christ." Philippians 1:6b

Dear Heavenly Father,

Thank You for your faithfulness. I choose to be an encouragement. I re-sign to live for You who died for me. I claim Your strength and rely on You to perform Your work in and through me. In Jesus' name, Amen.

Bible Reading – Galatians 6:1-10

Notes

____

____

____

____

____

____

____

PERSEVERE

BOTH HANDS FULL

"..with one of his hands wrought in the work, and with the other hand held a weapon. For the builders, everyone had his sword girded by his side, and so builded."

Nehemiah 4:17b - 18a

I cannot tell you how many times that my husband has asked, "Are you done with that schoolwork yet?"

"Are you kidding? This is just the tip of the iceberg," is one of my many responses.

He will teasingly sing, "It's the job that never ends. It goes on, and on my friend," to the tune of "The Song That Never Ends." Then we smile at each other as I wrap up another night of grading or developing lessons.

As teachers our job is rarely over when we leave school. Planning, creating lessons, developing modified work, completing student reports, grading, and so many other things can consume our thinking and time. We must learn to have a balanced life, or the enemy will take advantage. After all, he is "as a roaring lion…, seeking whom he may devour." (1 Peter 5:8b)

In Nehemiah, the Children of Israel were rebuilding the temple. At the same time, the enemies of God's people joined together to destroy them and their work. With prayer and new strategies put into place, they knew God's work had to be completed so there was no stopping. Aware of the forces against them, the workers started keeping a weapon in one hand and worked with a tool in the other. If the weapons weren't in their hands, their swords were girded at their sides ready to draw when necessary. The Israelites continued to build up the temple and were ready to fight the enemy.

As believers, we must not forget that we have a spiritual enemy. If we get consumed with the work of our calling and don't take measures to guard against the works of darkness, God's call and work in our life may fail. The sword is essential to warfare and, according to Paul, that is the Word of God. We cannot allow ourselves to be so busy with what God has called us to do that we ignore the Bible which is our spiritual weapon against the enemy. Take time daily to meditate on God's Word so that when you face challenges from students, colleagues, or parents that you will know how to respond in the Spirit. Keep one hand on the Sword while you influence and build students' minds with the other hand for Christ's sake.

"Study to shew thyself approved unto God, a workman that needeth not to be ashamed, rightly dividing the word of truth." 2 Timothy 2:15

Dear Heavenly Father,

Thank You for giving me the Word of God to protect and provide all that I need. I choose to keep Your Word in my heart so that as I teach and do my duties that I will withstand the wiles of the devil. May I always keep the Sword in one hand and work diligently with the other to please You. In Jesus' name, Amen.

Bible Reading – Nehemiah 4

NOTES

____

____

____

____

____

____

PERSEVERE
POWER IN CITATION

*"For the word of God is quick,
and powerful, and sharper than any
twoedged sword, ..."*

Hebrews 4:12a

"Let's review before we start your written response questions. Why is it important to cite your evidence?" I asked.

"It tells what the author says so it's not just my thoughts," one student replied.

"The text evidence helps support my thoughts about the topic," responded another student, "and can persuade my readers to agree with me."

In Matthew 4, Jesus cited Old Testament passages to stifle Satan's ploy to tempt Him after He prayed and fasted for forty days. Three times Jesus said, "It is written," and quoted scriptures. First, He cited that "every word that proceedeth out of the mouth of God" brings life. (vs. 4) He pointed Satan to the author, our

Creator. They were God's words not just Jesus' words. Next, Satan quoted some persuasive scriptures to tempt Jesus, and He rebutted, "It is said, Thou shalt not tempt the Lord thy God." (vs.7) Finally, Satan tried to get Jesus to worship him. His dedication to the Father was revealed by His prayer and fasting, so when He cited, "Thou shalt worship the Lord thy God, and him only shalt thou serve," (vs. 10) Jesus was supporting His heart's desire to serve the Father. With His final citation, Satan was persuaded that Jesus was not going to succumb to his temptations.

Jesus demonstrated there is power in citation of scriptures. Before we can cite Biblical evidence, we must read and glean from it. Our faith is built by hearing and reading the Word of God. Relying on the Author of our salvation to strengthen our faith through His Word is vital. The more we know of the Bible, the stronger our faith becomes. When we share our thoughts of faith, the Word of God should flow freely in harmony with them. Being convinced in our own hearts of the promises and admonitions in God's Word, can persuade and increase the appetite of others for the things of Christ. Read the Bible. Build your faith. Gather applicable passages to overcome trials and temptations. Cite His Word with confidence when given the opportunity. There is power in the Word of God!

"Looking unto Jesus the author and finisher of our faith..." Hebrews 12:2a

Dear Heavenly Father,

Thank You for Jesus Christ! As He spoke the Word of God in faith, help me to do the same. Forgive me for not taking time to read and study the Bible as I should. I cling to the words that You have for me and my family today. Help me recall scriptures when faced with temptations. As I cite Your words of truth, may they convince others to know You as their personal Lord. In Jesus' name, Amen.

Bible Reading – Matthew 4

NOTES

____

____

____

____

____

____

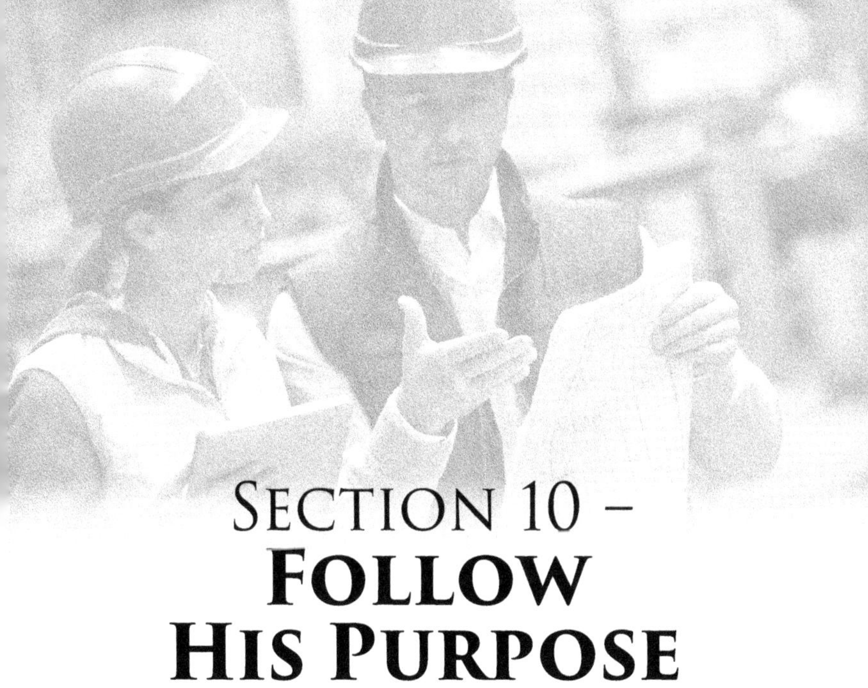

Section 10 – **Follow His Purpose**

Follow His Purpose

Ye Are the Light of the World

"Ye are the light of the world. A city that is set on an hill cannot be hid."

Matthew 5:14

For years, I was in a classroom that had no windows. It would get pitch black when lights were turned off, especially when we had practice lockdown drills. On one of our drills, we were packed on the floor in and around my desk. A boy said, "I can't see my hand!" Others chimed in, "Me either."

"Shhh. We're supposed to be quiet." I cautioned.

I heard a whimper. Then the sweet girl next to me began to sob and shake all over. She was terrified. I put my arms around her to calm her, but she didn't completely relax until I turned on my cellphone. It put off just enough light to make her feel safe again. We were all relieved when the classroom lights could be turned back on.

Our light can bring hope and relief to those around us. Adverse childhood experiences (ACEs) are more prevalent in our students today than ever. Less and less of our students come from stable homes, and they come to us with lots of baggage. Their life experiences have created fear, depression, aggression, lack of confidence, and many other side effects. Our students' world may be just like my pitch-dark classroom. As a Christian teacher, students need to experience a glimmer of hope through the light that we shine on them with kindness and patience. Our loving actions can preserve and will support the students that God has entrusted to us. It brings glory to our Heavenly Father when we shine for Him.

The small light from my cellphone gave off quite a bit of light in that pitch black corner. Our world is a dark place where fear, anxiety, and distrust rules. As Christians, we are the lights, the candles, that may bring just enough light for others to have hope and to find Christ. Jesus tells us that He is the light of the world, and John encourages us to "...walk in the light as he is in the light..." (1 John 1:7) Paul in Ephesians tells us to "...walk as children of light:" (Ephesians 5:8) Let's be the light that shines on darkness and brings peace to the troubled soul. Our daily walk should reflect the light of the world, Jesus. Let Him shine!

"Let your light so shine before men, that they may see your good works, and glorify your Father which is in heaven." Matthew 5:16

Dear Heavenly Father,

Thank You for being the Light that has brought me hope and freedom. Help me to let my light shine brightly that others may experience hope in You. Help me today and every day to walk in You. As the song says, "This little light of mine, I'm going to let it shine." I choose to shine and shine and shine for your honor and your glory. In Jesus' name that I pray. Amen.

Bible Reading – Matthew 5:1-16

Notes

Follow His Purpose

God's Schooling

"That the Lord thy God may shew us the way wherein we may walk, and the thing that we may do."

Jeremiah 42:3

"Does it get any easier? I thought last year was tough, but this year was even more challenging," said an exasperated young colleague.

I hesitated for a minute and responded, "No, it doesn't get easier. Every year brings challenges. It is hard work, however, there is satisfaction running your class with your own spin. Find what works for you and stick with it. Enjoy your students and the relationships that you build."

At each stage of his life, Moses learned from his encounters which helped him grow into one of the greatest leaders in biblical history. During his first forty years, he learned the laws of God from his mother and father before he was taken to the palace of Pharaoh.

There he learned the traditions and formalities of the Egyptians, including that of a prince. From 41 through 80 years old, Moses lived on the backside of the desert as a shepherd for his father-in-law. At the age of 80, God called Moses to lead the Israelites out of slavery. God had schooled him in all phases of his life in preparation of his leadership role. Moses recognized God's voice because of the lessons his parent had taught him at a young age. Moses learned the ways of the Egyptians when he lived in the palace, so he knew the appropriate ways to approach Pharaoh. Moses became acquainted with the lifestyle of a nomad and shepherd on the backside of the desert which was beneficial when he led the people through the wilderness. Each stage of Moses' life was difficult; however, he was able to use all his experiences and faith in God to successfully lead the Israelites.

The tough times in the classroom can benefit us if we choose to learn from them. Figuring out how to operate our classes more efficiently comes from the good and bad experiences. Leaning on Jesus as we face the challenges strengthens our faith and enables us to face new challenges. God's schooling comes in many different forms and is specific to His plan for each of us. Since the Great Teacher is leading in the instruction, we can trust He knows what's best for His desired outcome in our lives.

"I will instruct thee and teach thee in the way which thou shalt go: I will guide thee with mine eye." Psalm 32:8

Dear Heavenly Father,

Thank You for using all things to teach and guide me. Forgive me when I complain about the challenges in my class. May I learn from You and use my experiences to improve my walk with You. I surrender to being a teacher leader as You guide me. In Jesus' name, Amen.

Bible Reading – Exodus 3

NOTES

____

____

____

____

____

____

____

____

Follow His Purpose

God's Blueprints

"Therefore whosoever heareth these sayings of mine, and doeth them, I will liken him unto a wise man, which built his house upon a rock:"

Matthew 7:24

Good lesson plans include standards, objectives, strategies, and some form of evaluation. Focusing on standards and objectives are building blocks that lead to student success across grade levels. While strategies and evaluations focus on specific activity details needed to guide and meet individual needs, God's blueprints do the same for us.

God used dreams in Joseph's life to reveal a snapshot of the blueprints He had for Joseph and his family. His dreams were not well received. Joseph's life included being thrown into a pit by his brothers, sold as a servant twice, and then thrown into prison for something he didn't do. We may think, *"Surely God didn't plan for all of that to happen."* But He did! It was

Joseph's own confession to his brothers that confirmed God's blueprint: "Fear not: for am I in the place of God? ....ye thought evil against me; but God meant it unto good, to bring to pass, as it is this day, to save much people alive." (Genesis 50:19-20) God raised Joseph from the dungeon to be second in command to Pharaoh at His designed time and just as it was drawn up on His blueprints to preserve His people.

God has a blueprint for each of us. As our architect, Christ Jesus knows our specific needs, traits, and passions and has drawn up His plans for our life. As our engineer, God has created the perfect design for us to withstand all storms and hazards. When the storms of life come, I can't help but wonder if we alter His blueprints by trying to escape and work things out for ourselves. We make modifications to God's plans when we exclude Him in our decisions and/or seek our own pleasure. Christ may have drawn up the floor plan for a mansion, and we may be building a shack because we aren't following the specifications of His blueprints in our life. We need to remember that we are His workmanship (Ephesians 2:10) and belong to Him.

As the great architect and engineer of our life, He has designed and provided a secure plan through His Word to weather the storms without us altering His flawless plan. Let's build our life with Christ as the foundation and follow the specifications of His uniquely planned blueprints for our lives.

"... as a wise masterbuilder, I have laid the foundation, and another buildeth thereon. But let every man take heed how he buildeth thereupon." 1 Corinthians 3:10b

Dear Heavenly Father,

Thank You for having a blueprint specifically for me. I'm so grateful for the privilege of teaching. I am confident that I am following Your plan. Help me to keep my faith in You and not to alter Your plan. Help me to continue to follow Your blueprint for my life. I trust You. In Jesus' name, Amen.

Bible Reading – Genesis 37

NOTES

Follow His Purpose

People Are Reading Our Story

"Ye are our epistle written in our hearts, known and read of all men:"

2 Corinthians 3:2

Writing narratives is difficult for students. They introduce the characters, setting, problem, and solution but tend to leave out details of the rising action. They want to solve the problem as quickly as possible in their story. However, the twists and turns of the rising action help define the main character. Without those details, the story is underdeveloped and many times not realistic or interesting.

Our life story is being written as we live it. Just like the students we would prefer to bypass the twists and turns of our story. If possible, we would choose the easiest path, without considering how the conflicts in our life help us grow in Christ Jesus. The suspense and trials cause discomfort and often demand our actions. Those are the moments that define and build our character traits. As a believer, will we respond in faith or waver? If we falter, do we learn from that failure and seek God's forgiveness and will? If we are successful, do we praise God for the grace we have to endure? Are the details of our actions keeping the interest of our readers or have they lost interest in our spoken faith?

Just as Paul read the lives of the Corinthians as a letter, people are reading our story too. Our students, our family, our friends, our colleagues, and others are watching us as our storyline unfolds. We will not live a life without failures, but it is our response that reveals our true colors. A prayer to the Lord for forgiveness is a start. An apology to the offended one preaches volumes. Using kind words or no words when circumstances could provoke us is Godlike. A smile or a negative attitude being displayed amid your trouble is being read. Just as in a narrative, dialogue is less effective when it lacks narration that shows the action of the character. Our character traits are analyzed by our walk and our talk. It is the pattern of godliness or ungodliness in our lives that reveals whether our faith in God is genuine. We are an open book that has a theme. Will the lesson learned by our personal life story draw others to Christ or cause them to question Him?

"In all things shewing thyself a pattern of good works: in doctrine shewing uncorruptness, gravity, sincerity," Titus 2:7

Dear Heavenly Father,

Thank You for Your life story. Your perfect example and sacrifice on Calvary have provided all that I need in this life. Forgive me when I fail to meet my trials in faith. I choose to face each challenge with actions and words that please You above all else. As my story is being written and read by others, may they be drawn to know You, my Savior, and my God. In Jesus' name, Amen.

Bible Reading – Jonah 1 & 2

NOTES

Bonus:
Prayers & Poetry

PRECIOUS HEAVENLY FATHER,

Thank You for giving me the ministry of teaching children. You have given me a passion to teach, to love, and cherish those whom I have the privilege to teach. I am grateful for a new school year to make a difference in children's lives. Looking beyond the challenges of COVID-19 and other concerns in our community, I ask that You help me to stay focused on Your calling for my life – bestowing wisdom and knowledge, building relationships, and being a good Christian role model.

I uplift our administrators and teacher leaders and ask that You give them discernment and understanding. Help them to patiently work together for the good of our staff and students. With turmoil all around, I ask that You calm the storm and provide Your indescribable peace and tranquility. Help us all to lean hard on You, Lord Jesus, and walk in faith, not in fear.

I pray for my colleagues. Create in us a unity that resonates in our hallways. May we uplift and encourage one another. Help us to guard our words and be sensitive to each other. May we join together to create lessons, units, and programs that will have a positive impact on our students and families. Remind us to pray for each other daily for Your name's sake.

I submit my life afresh to You and trust that my teaching will please You above all else. As I teach students the standards set before me, help me to educate with a zeal that will kindle their interest to become lifelong learners. Give me the energy needed to meet the day-to-day challenges whether academic, emotional, or personal. May all my students sense Your perfect love in the way that I behave myself toward them.

I release my requests to You and trust that You know what is best for my life and those that I care about. Bless and protect us. I humbly submit my petitions to You and accept Your perfect will this day!

In Christ's name I pray, Amen.

Pray a Scripture for Someone
Ephesians 3:16-21

Our school days can be so chaotic that it is difficult to touch base with our colleagues and friends. Without communicating, it can be difficult to know how or what to pray. Although, this pray is not specific, it is all encompassing.

Dear Heavenly Father,

I ask you to grant _________ all the resources that she/he needs today according to your glory and for your honor. Please, give him/her strength by your power and might expressly by the Holy Spirit touching him/her to the innermost. May ___________ be assured that your Son dwells in his/her heart by having faith in what you have done for him/her. Help _______ to be rooted and grounded in heavenly love. May he/she be able to truly comprehend the breadth, length, depth, and height of your capabilities to meet his/her every need. Provide ____ with experiences that portray the absolute love of Christ Jesus which surpasses all other. Flood his/her heart and soul with the fullness of God and His goodness. Remind him/her that you are able to do exceeding, abundantly, above all that she/he asks or even thinks because of the power of Christ that works in and through him/her as a believer. I thank you for being the God that you are and trust you on __________'s behalf today. Be honored and glorified.

In Christ's precious name,

Amen

In essence this prayer of faith is seeking.

- resources to meet each need for the glory of God
- strength from the Holy Spirit that has touched the inner man (spirit & soul)
- assurance of salvation the dwells in the heart by faith in Christ Jesus
- love that is rooted and grounded (secure & true)
- the understanding of how powerful God really is (all dimensions)

- a heart and soul that is saturated with God and His goodness
- the Creator God who answers above and beyond what is asked or thought of

*This prayer says it all. It focuses on the Savior and not on the problem or need. God is able!

Dear Heavenly Father,

Thank you for hearing my prayers. In Jesus' name, Amen.

PRAYER BEFORE STATE TESTING

Precious Heavenly Father,

Thank You for giving me the ministry of teaching children. You have given me a passion to teach, love and cherish those whom I have the privilege to teach. I am grateful for the opportunity to make a difference in children's life daily. Looking beyond the challenges in the world of education, I ask that You help me to stay focused on Your calling for my life – bestowing wisdom and knowledge, building relationships, and being a good Christian role model.

The state may try to judge my teaching by standardized tests, but I know that ultimately You are my judge. I trust that my teaching meets Your expectations, and I choose to please You above all else. As I teach students the standards set before me, help me to educate with a zeal that will kindle their interest to become lifelong learners. Give me the energy needed to meet the daily challenges whether academic, emotional, or personal. May all my students sense Your perfect love in the way that I behave myself toward them.

As the state assessments approach, I ask that You bring to remembrance the lessons that have been taught to my students as well to the students of my dear friends. I pray that each child will feel empowered to answer questions correctly or at least to the best of their ability. Please reward my efforts along with my fellow teacher friends with high student achievement. May the growth that has been witnessed in the classroom be apparent on the statewide test.

I release my requests to You and trust that You know what is best for my life and those that I care about. Bless our students. I humbly submit my petitions to You and accept Your perfect will!

In Christ's name I pray, Amen.

Grateful to the Father

I'm so grateful for the Father's love,
Who sent his Son Jesus from Heaven above.
To die for me, for my sin debt to pay
Regardless of what many think or say
It took Christ's blood to wash my sins away.
So I forsook my sins and set out to live,
A life to please Jesus which is all I could give.

I'm so grateful to the Father above.
Christ was our example in how we should love.
He not only gave His life for you and me,
But He saved, healed, and delivered for all to see,
His mercy endures for all to believe.
One must come to Him, accept Him, and receive
The love of the Savior so rich and free.

Are you grateful to the Father from above?
Have you allowed Him to shower you with His love?
Christ is waiting for you to give Him your life.
Forsake and confess all selfishness and strife.
Once you have taken Him as your Savior and friend.
You will find you can trust Him and upon Him depend.
He will guide you and comfort you to the very end.

It's All About the Gift

There is a good and perfect gift!
Jesus came from Heav'n above.
To love, to save, and completely uplift
Those who will receive his gift of love

He was born in a barn of lowly estate.
He was wrapped in swaddling clothes.
Jesus was his name, the angels relayed
To the shepherds as they began to doze.

The wise men came with gifts from afar.
To worship and praise His name
His birth was affirmed by that easterly star.
They had studied and had to proclaim.

Jesus is the greatest gift of all!
His salvation free for you who believe
Forgiveness and peace for those who call
On His sweet name, his free gift to receive

Do you know Jesus, the gift of God?
Have you received Him as your own?
Are you living a life for Him to applaud?
Will He say, "Well done" at His throne?

Biblical References:

<u>James 1:17</u> "Every good gift and every perfect gift is from above, and cometh down from the Father of lights, with whom is no variableness, neither shadow of turning."

<u>John 3:16</u> "For God so loved the world, that he gave his only begotten Son, that whosoever believeth in him should not perish, but have everlasting life."

<u>John 4:10</u> "Jesus answered and said unto her, If thou knewest the gift of God, and who it is that saith to thee, Give me to drink; thou wouldest have asked of him, and he would have given thee living water."

<u>Romans 6:23</u> "For the wages of sin is death; but the gift of God is eternal life through Jesus Christ our Lord."

<u>2 Corinthians 9:15</u> "Thanks be unto God for his unspeakable gift."

<u>John 1:12</u> "But as many as received him, to them gave he power to become the sons of God, even to them that believe on his name:"

Whose Birthday Is It Anyway?

I can just imagine Jesus looking on this
Christmas day,
And asking God the Father, whose
birthday is it anyway?
Don't they remember that I'm the one
this day is all about?
Many who are receiving gifts have
forgotten me, no doubt.

I came to Earth from Heaven their sin debt to pay.
The Virgin Mary gave birth to me on God's
appointed day.
Why is so much money spent for others to
receive gifts?
When it is my birthday and my name they
should uplift.

The angels with praise announced my birth on
that night.
Shepherds came to worship me in the manger
with delight.
They left with such excitement to tell others
of my birth.
Consider me this Christmas and worship me
with mirth.

The wise men came from a distance with gifts of
great worth.
They followed the star from the east to celebrate my birth.
They gave me gold, frankincense, and myrrh their
love to display.
They set a good example of how to celebrate me on
my birthday.

Remember me with gifts of praise and teach others
of my fame.
I sacrificed myself for you. Please don't
forget my name.
Show me you remember. Give your life afresh to
me this day.
Include me in your Christmas joy. Whose birthday is
it anyway?

More About the Author

Dru Cox Pearcy has been a Christian for over fifty years. Her father was her pastor and mentor for over forty years. She learned from her father, as pastor and counselor, to listen intently, consider God's principles in every situation, then draw from the Word of God and apply it to all aspects of life. Her father passed away in 2007. Now her husband is pastor, and together they have had the privilege of ministering to their small congregation.

From a young child, Dru believed God's calling was for her to be a missionary. She wanted to reach others for Christ and by fourth grade Dru knew that she wanted to be a teacher. As time came for her to graduate from high school, she had a deep conversation with her parents about both passions. Dru loved teaching Sunday school and vacation Bible school, so she had a passion for teaching, but she wanted to be a missionary too. After praying for a few days together with her parents, her father made a profound statement to her, "Missionaries come in all forms. Can't you be a missionary in public schools?" God gave Dru peace, and she knew God's calling and mission was to teach.

Dru had a bit of a detour though. She and her husband, Matt, started their family. She decided to stay home with her children which allowed her to teach weekday religious education for the local schools for twelve years. After Dru had her third daughter, her mother encouraged her to substitute teach, so she could pursue her teaching career. Her mother would be her babysitter. That didn't last long. Dru's mother was diagnosed with cancer and died within six months. Her babysitter (best friend) was gone. As a stay-at-home mom, she became the babysitter for her brother and sister's children. Now with five of her own and six of theirs, she was quite busy. As Dru's youngest daughter turned five years old, she knew she needed to help support the family financially. Dru considered different options, but God tapped her on the shoulder and reminded her of His calling for her life – a teacher.

Dru interviewed for the first time in her life at the age of 38, and God provided her a fourth-grade teaching position. She has completed over 22 years of teaching as a fourth and fifth grade teacher in three different buildings in the same corporation. God has blessed Dru. She has been recognized by her colleagues in each of those buildings as their "Teacher of the Year" candidate. To God be the glory!

For the past fifteen years, Dru has led small groups of teachers and staff members with brief devotionals and prayer time. Ten years ago, Dru began writing her own thoughts and sharing them with her small group. That group of teachers encouraged her to write a book. After speaking to an editor of books, she determined to start a blog "Dru's Inspirational Writings" instead. This past year, Dru attended a conference where those in attendance were encouraged by Dr. David Jeremiah to take risks and push forward for God's sake. Dru determined to use her teaching experience and Bible knowledge to write for Christ's sake with a desire to encourage fellow believer teachers.

Education: Bachelor of Science K-6 Teacher's Degree from Indiana State University – 1981, Master of Education from Indiana Wesleyan University – 2008.

Personal: Parade All American & Indiana All-Star in Basketball 1977, Indiana Track & Field three-time state champion in softball throw 1975-1977, ISU Basketball 1977-1980, Indiana Basketball Hall of Fame 2004, Indiana Track & Cross Country Hall of Fame 2021, Plainfield High School Hall of Fame 2021

CPSIA information can be obtained
at www.ICGtesting.com
Printed in the USA
BVHW091913160822
644714BV00008B/543